TEACHING WHERE YOU ARE

Teaching Where You Are

Weaving Indigenous and Slow Principles and Pedagogies

SHANNON LEDDY AND LORRIE MILLER

UNIVERSITY OF TORONTO PRESS
Toronto Buffalo London

© University of Toronto Press 2024
Toronto Buffalo London
utorontopress.com
Printed and bound by CPI Group (UK) Ltd, Croydon, CR0 4YY

ISBN 978-1-4875-4994-7 (cloth)   ISBN 978-1-4875-4995-4 (EPUB)
ISBN 978-1-4875-5401-9 (paper)   ISBN 978-1-4875-4996-1 (PDF)

Library and Archives Canada Cataloguing in Publication

Title: Teaching where you are : weaving Indigenous and slow principles and
    pedagogies / Shannon Leddy and Lorrie Miller.
Names: Leddy, Shannon, author. | Miller, Lorrie, author.
Description: Includes bibliographical references and index.
Identifiers: Canadiana (print) 20230483747 | Canadiana (ebook) 20230483771 |
    ISBN 9781487549947 (hardcover) | ISBN 9781487554019 (softcover) |
    ISBN 9781487549954 (EPUB) | ISBN 9781487549961 (PDF)
Subjects: LCSH: Culturally relevant pedagogy. | LCSH: Culturally sustaining
    pedagogy. | LCSH: Experiential learning. | LCSH: Curriculum change. |
    LCSH: Indigenous peoples – Education. | LCSH: Social justice and education.
Classification: LCC LC1099.515.C85 L43 2024 | DDC 370.117 – dc24

Cover design: EmDash Design
Cover image: Lorrie Miller

We wish to acknowledge the land on which the University of Toronto Press
operates. This land is the traditional territory of the Wendat, the Anishnaabeg, the
Haudenosaunee, the Métis, and the Mississaugas of the Credit First Nation.

This book has been published with the help of a grant from the Federation for the
Humanities and Social Sciences, through the Awards to Scholarly Publications
Program, using funds provided by the Social Sciences and Humanities Research
Council of Canada.

University of Toronto Press acknowledges the financial support of the Government
of Canada, the Canada Council for the Arts, and the Ontario Arts Council, an agency
of the Government of Ontario, for its publishing activities.

Canada Council   Conseil des Arts
for the Arts   du Canada

ONTARIO ARTS COUNCIL
CONSEIL DES ARTS DE L'ONTARIO
an Ontario government agency
un organisme du gouvernement de l'Ontario

Funded by the   Financé par le
Government   gouvernement
of Canada   du Canada   Canada

We dedicate this book to all of the children who dream of learning, and to all the teachers who seek to guide them with good hearts and good minds. Kimaskisiwin. You are strong.

To serve others, to be of some use to family, community, nation or the world is one of the main purposes for which human beings have been created. Do not fill yourself with your own affairs and forget your most important task. True happiness comes only to those who have dedicated their lives to the service of others.

– *The Sacred Tree*, Philip Lane Jr., Lee Brown,
Judy Bopp and Michael Bopp (1984, p. 81)

We are one spirit, one song, and our world will be harmonious only when we make the time to care. For ourselves. For each other. For our home. You don't need to be a Native person to understand that – just human.

– *One Drum: Stories and Ceremonies for a Planet*,
Richard Wagamese (2019, p. 37)

Contents

Illustrations

Abbreviations

ACDE	Association of Canadian Deans of Education
CTF	Canadian Teachers' Federation
FNESC	First Nations Education Steering Committee
FPPoL	First Peoples Principles of Learning
IRS	Indian Residential School
MMWIG	Missing and Murdered Indigenous Women and Girls
TRC	Truth and Reconciliation Commission
UNDRIP	United Nations Declaration on the Rights of Indigenous Peoples

Weaving and Reweaving Indigenous Education in New Ways through the Timelessness of Transformative Thought, Teaching, and Learning

Someone once asked, "what is Indigenous education?" As an educator of Woodland Cree heritage who has been in the field for over twenty years, I would reply that it is the *same education* as the wolves that occupy the Northern Saskatchewan context where I come from. It is the same education as the bears. It is the same education as the ravens, eagles, foxes, weasels, fish, and our medicines that keep us healthy. Creator provided the natural world with original instructions that make us who we are in all of our diversity. We are inseparable from the land, plants, and animals that share our existence. We are inseparable from the Spirit world where time does not exist. The ebb and flow of life has its own timing and cyclical order from which we learn natural laws and spiritual laws. In the Circle there is no beginning and no end. Only the mysterious dance of life that happens in the messiness of schooling.

Teaching and learning from Indigenous perspectives means a shift in thinking that requires teachers and pre-service teachers to unpack and lay down what they have learned on a blanket. Colourful threads, beads, and gems of Indigenous wisdom, ready to be weaved, require tools, skills, and the voices of Indigenous Knowledge Keepers and teachers that transcend time and space. Tobacco is offered as protocol, and we do what we are supposed to do when the timing is right. There is no prepackaged curriculum that works in all contexts. *Teaching Where You Are: Weaving Indigenous and Slow Principles and Pedagogies* by

Dr. Shannon Leddy and Dr. Lorrie Miller is a must read that highlights the parallel between Indigenous ways of knowing and the pedagogical concept of *slow learning*. There are eight chapters altogether, shared in the most eloquent, holistic, and circular narrative of the Medicine Wheel symbolic system.

Elders say there is a time and place for everything. It's not right to live such a rigid life. Stress sets in and teachers burn out. Learning happens on its own time frame. Learning most certainly happens beyond the "clock time" of schools. The concept of lifelong learning is embedded in Indigenous thought. Sometimes seeds of thought are planted when we are not ready to receive the knowledge. Even twenty years down the road, we finally get it. We finally realize that we were being taught something without realizing it at the time. This happens quite often, for example, in Indigenous storytelling methodology where the teacher becomes the artist in the creation of a particular message. In this book, Leddy and Miller introduce themselves as teachers first and then their specialization in art education, where they both know that artists are led by a *creation force* that crosses physical and spiritual worlds to teach us life lessons.

The first chapter of the book is the hook that captures my attention. Indigenous and non-Indigenous educators working together, sharing their knowledge, and weaving words of wisdom to create a teacher-friendly resource that challenges "clock time" in teaching and learning. The reworking and reweaving of curriculum in thought and practice requires *relational* and *reciprocal* ways of doing things to reach students at the right time and right place. Not everyone learns the same way nor at the same pace. This must be respected in a sacred way. The Indigenous *ethic of non-interference* is used by Indigenous Knowledge Keepers quite often so that students are able to explore, learn, and take ownership of their own learning. Elders say each child is "special sent" from the Spirit world to make contributions in families, communities, and Nations. Sometimes a child is an "old soul" full of knowledge. They have something to teach us if we only take the *time* to listen.

The fluidity of *timelessness* is best experienced on the land. Time collapses when past, present, and future come together in the discourse of Indigenous education. The changing of the seasons come and go. We live by the cycle of the sun. We greet the morning as it begins to emerge from the Eastern doorway. We travel into other realms of existence in our dream world where there is no time. Trickster in our origin stories teach us about continuous flux, change, and transformation. We did certain things at certain times of the year. Knowledge is passed down when we are ready to receive it. Our cultural life ways and languages are rooted in the lands and waters we occupy. Land-based education is taking shape across the country against a social and historical backdrop of colonization and residential schools. Teachers not only teach for the sake of teaching, but they also have to deal with historical trauma in schools and places of higher learning. Sometimes they lack the techniques and the background knowledge of the intergenerational impacts of residential schools. Leddy and Miller, like other educators, believe healing from trauma is about *process*, which flows according to its own timing. Teacher educators, teachers, and pre-service teachers, whether they are Indigenous or non-Indigenous, will have continuous questions of teaching and learning as theories and practice change.

I am honoured to have reviewed the book manuscript. The writing is captivating and rich with metaphor and scholarly thought. There are links to the work of Indigenous scholars across the country and abroad. It is most definitely a *weaved* regalia full of life and vibrancy as it sets the foundation for other work to come from the teachers and pre-service teachers that Dr. Shannon Leddy and Dr. Lori Miller are working with at the University of British Columbia and other places of higher learning. They weave together their past teacher experiences in First Nations and Métis communities and acknowledge the Knowledge Keepers that have taught them to think of time in Indigenous ways.

In this book, you will notice *collective thought* and *collective consciousness* and most importantly a *collective weaving* of theory and practice. I ask readers to engage in deep thinking about teaching and learning in a post-colonial world that is still reeling from the residual impacts of the educational silencing of Indigenous peoples. The uncovering of what lays beneath the blanket of the *Great White Winter* is emerging into a springtime – a re-awakening of new thought, new conceptualizations, and new ways of doing things in our schools. Indigenous education benefits all teachers and learners regardless of race, class, gender, ethnicity, and other social markers.

Herman Michell, PhD

Preface

It's funny how we find our ways in the world, walking our pathways, laying down trails, and crossing paths with others as we travel through the days. The authors, Lorrie and Shannon, first met around 2008 or 2009, while Shannon was still a high school teacher, and Lorrie was working in adult education, alongside an active practice as a writer and editor. Little did we know then how closely paralleled our paths were, much less how they would finally cross again ten years later in the Faculty of Education at UBC, where we now both work. Those first few conversations about writing over a decade ago have now blossomed into this book, and we couldn't be more pleased to share it with you.

After reconnecting and finding that we shared even more interests and ideas in common than we initially realized, we began to actively find ways to write and present together and share our understanding of the importance of decolonizing curriculum and indigenizing pedagogy. In early 2019, we got together to present at the annual meeting of the American Educational Research Association in Toronto, Ontario. During the development of our presentation and the discussions at that meeting, the seed for this book was planted. We agreed we were seeing too many frazzled teacher candidates in our offices, and we were feeling the academy's pressure cooker impact on their well-being and our own. We knew that there must be a way to do things differently. We sketched out our ideas and then got down to writing over the following year, working independently and then sharing our work over cups of coffee, lunches, and afternoon beverages at patios around town. The two quotes we placed at the start of this text as an epigraph embody the spirit in which we worked together. We truly wish to "serve others, to be of some use ..." (Lane et. al., 1984, p. 81) because we know what is possible "when we take the time to care ..." (Wagamese, 2019, p. 37). We hope that you read this text with that spirit in mind.

Lorrie is a practicing and talented textile artist who brings a wealth of knowledge and experience to her textile classes, including philosophical considerations around the impact of commercial textile production and the labour involved in traditional production methods. Her curriculum touches on history, sustainability, biology, mathematics, design, and chemistry, and raises the same concerns that Shannon brings to her work in Indigenous education. Moreover, Lorrie has come to understand the value of doing things slowly, and nurtures in her students the principle that sometimes things must be undone to be done again correctly.

Shannon is also an artist with a modest body of painted and sculptural work. As a teacher, thinking like an artist has allowed her to make the same broad curricular connections that Lorrie brings to her work. Over the past twenty years, since meeting her birth father and being able to give a name to the Indigenous Nation she is from (Métis), Shannon has dedicated her teaching career to including the Indigenous ways of knowing that were shared with her as a young person in Saskatoon. As a scholar, she looks to the work of Indigenous researchers, educators, and activists to help students see how Canadian curricula have functioned to silence Indigenous voices and why it is crucial to bring those voices to the fore. None of our work can be done without the efforts of those who have come before and paved the way. We stand on the shoulders of giants.

As soon as the work commenced, we recognized that we had made an excellent team. Where Lorrie brought her focus on Slow pedagogy to these pages, Shannon attended to Indigenous pedagogies, and both authors worked hard to highlight the ways in which these two approaches parallel and complement one another. Things were taking shape ... and then COVID-19 hit and added yet another context to consider in our writing. Following that, the grim discovery of the 215 unmarked graves of school children at the former Kamloops Indian Residential School (IRS) was revealed to the world, followed by more in sites throughout Western Canada. As teachers, we recognize the need to be responsive to our students' emergent needs and concerns, meet them where they are, and dare to name the elephant in the room. We found that to do justice to our original ideas, we also needed to consider the weight and impact of these key events in our work.

In writing a book about Indigenous and Slow pedagogies, we feel that our process should also be transparent to remove the mystery of how a text is created and help the reader trace how we have formed our considerations and reconsiderations as we worked. This creative and critical process should also reflect the ways of working that we are espousing. Things take as long as they take, and not everything can be rushed. So, we have taken our time to develop the ideas in these pages and turned to critical friends for feedback on our work in progress. It felt both risky and safe. Indigenous and Slow ways call for the involvement of others as we learn from the insights and wisdom of Elders, Knowledge-Keepers, teachers, and constructively critical friends. Collaboration is honoured and preferred in our work; we engaged in writing together, trading chapters back and forth so that we each had input into each section of the manuscript and invited several trusted colleagues into our process to act as sounding boards and devil's advocates to improve and deepen our work. We are deeply grateful for the critical feedback and support we received from these early readers, and from editors at the University of Toronto Press, and hope our revisions have done their feedback justice.

During this time, we also explored the notion of sister-scholarship and carried with us the idea of a more compassionate and non-competitive way of doing scholarship. Our personal lives turned corners as we dealt with career moves, illness, family growth and loss, selling and buying houses, moving, and a global pandemic. Our writing is in our lives, and our lives are in our writing. There is no separation of the two. We hope that this intentionality in our text brings our readers to a more balanced and relational way of teaching and learning that includes both Indigenous and Western ways of thinking and knowing. We have structured our text to maximize its appeal to educators at all stages of their careers, from teacher candidates and novice teachers to those working in teacher education. We offer our thoughts with the spirit of the seven sacred teachings in our hearts: Love, Truth, Courage, Humility, Honesty, Wisdom, and Respect. We hope that you will receive them with the good spirit they were intended.

Acknowledgements

Along with the personal acknowledgements we will make, we want to ensure that the Critical Friends mentioned in our preface are highlighted. Upon completing our first draft, we sent our work out to several Indigenous educators and in-service teachers to get a sense of how close we were to our target. Thanks to their thoughtful reading and feedback, we were able to push ourselves deeper in several vital directions and draw further on their wisdom and experiences to strengthen our work. Our profound gratitude goes out to Kau'i Keliipio, Jo Chrona, Dr. Amber Shilling, and Jean Quon for their generosity and critical guidance.

Our sincere thanks go to our editor, Meg Patterson. She saw value in our ideas and worked so hard to guide, nurture, and inspire us throughout this project. She and the team at the University of Toronto Press have made the publication of this manuscript possible, and we owe them a deep debt of gratitude for all they have done to help us realize this dream.

We are also deeply grateful to our families and colleagues who cheered us along as we completed this work. It took many long hours of research, writing, revising, and thinking to bring our ideas together in a good way, and we have so many people to thank for their patience while we attended to getting it all done. Without their care, kindness, constancy and love, we could never have seen the job through. Kinaniskomitin!!

Lorrie Miller's acknowledgements: Above all, I thank my sister-scholar Shannon for her vision, tenacity, scholarship, humour, and the amazing ability to say it like it is. It has been a profound honour to work with you on this book.

I would like to thank the students and parents from Pukatawagan, Manitoba, who launched this young art teacher over three decades ago onto a rich journey of learnings never expected. Thank you to Dr. Rita Irwin, who guided me further along my academic journey, and Dr. Kit Grauer, who showed me just how fun textile art education can be. I am blessed to now teach the class she once taught me.

I thank my children, Akask, Wolfgang, Chloe, and Finnleigh for the curiosity, care, and balance they bring to my life outside of work, and my young granddaughter Inanna, who exemplifies why this work is needed. I also thank Graham Coleman, who has been my pillar of strength, an open ear, a kind critic, and a fabulous skipper. I could not have done any of this without his support.

Shannon Leddy's acknowledgements: I wish to thank so many teachers and mentors who have guided me in my own learning journey over the years. The late, great Dr. Cheryl Meszaros, Mr. John Perret, Mrs. Paula Grudic, the late Dr. Robert Williamson, Dr. Susan O'Neill, Dr. Dolores van der Wey, Dr. Vicky Kelly, Dr. Michelle Pidgeon, Elder Dorothy Visser, Dr. Eduardo Jovel, Dr. Alannah Young, Dan Kane and the whole Kane clan, and Eileen Leddy (my very first teacher) are just a few of those whom I wish to thank. Most importantly, I thank my wise-beyond-his-years son, Ben, for his kind, loving patience and putting up with his mother's occasional weirdness, and my partner Andy, for his constant love and for sharing every day in the best conversation I have ever had.

1

Tawâw

Tawâw is the Nehiyaw Cree word for welcome. But it means so much more than that – it also means *there is room for you here*, and *it is open*. We chose this word to begin our book because we hope it will evoke the feeling of invitation that we wish to convey. We welcome you to enter this book as a dialogue with us. So, come on in, just as you are, settle down with some tea, and join us all in the work we are here to do together!

Here, our introduction is a roadmap through this text for readers. We intend to make evident the parallels between Slow pedagogy, with which many non-Indigenous people are already familiar, and the many Indigenous pedagogies and ways of knowing. While these two approaches are similar and complementary, they are also rooted in different ontologies and different ways of seeing the world, which will inform our work. In setting the stage for this work, we introduce our narrative tone with the voices and stories of both authors and bring into focus the central theme at the heart of this book: education as a human endeavour, holistic and transformative, in a time of decolonization, climate crisis, global pandemic, and super-connectivity. Indigenous perspectives are critical here because, as Marie Battiste (2000) has pointed out, the reason to include Indigenous pedagogies, knowledges (with permission), and ways of knowing in educational practice "is not [so] that Aboriginal students can compete with non-Aboriginal students in an imagined world. It is, rather, that

Figure 1.1. Medicine Wheel, 2018.

Source: Courtesy of Shannon Leddy.

immigrant society is sorely in need of what Aboriginal knowledge has to offer" (p. 201).

After this introductory chapter, the central chapters are designed to be read in any order, much like the Medicine Wheel (figure 1.1), circular – with no beginning nor end. We will also be weaving our ideas together, and to make good use of this metaphor, we will be turning to the language and practices of weaving. We hope this text will be of use to teacher educators and their pre-service teachers in helping them connect and unpack their own school experiences in relation to thinking about how to include Indigenous ways of teaching, learning, and knowing. We hope in-service teachers will find this book useful to fill in some of the gaps that may have been left during their teacher education days, helping them meld their tried-and-true classroom methods with Indigenous pedagogical approaches and resources.

~

A clock is a clock, is a clock. It knows what time it is, but it does not care. It cannot. Yet, we know that the time we *spend* never seems to be enough to get all things done, and we would do so much more if we just had more time. It is both a luxury and a commodity. Though an object and symbol of time, it does not tell us about our era – the times of reconciliation, the climate crisis, hyper-connectivity, and intentionally addictive technology and social media platforms. A clock does not have an alarm to tell you when enough is enough.

Historically, a clock has also been a mechanism used to impose Western values and definitions of productivity connected to agricultural practices and commerce. Clocks disrupted Indigenous ways of knowing and being by breaking the natural rhythm of seasonal and cyclical time that successfully guided us for centuries. As Donald Fixico (2003) has phrased it, the "focus on events and stories about them has deemphasized the measuring of time on the clock of the linear world. To [I]ndigenous people, the hands of the white man's clock sometimes feel wrapped around the person's throat, strangling the soul from being free and dictating one's life by deadlines" (pp. 50–1). Despite this insidious disconnection, there are still relationships between Western and Indigenous ideas of time. For example, in the Northern hemisphere, our notions of a "clockwise direction" are based on the path of the sun, and also apply to both clocks and Medicine Wheels.

The central question of our era resides in the valuation of things that cannot be counted. Many of us, it would seem, are looking broadly at finding meaning in our lives that transcends the simple accumulation of stuff. This is critical, as it is abundantly clear that our planet cannot sustain *more* things. This book explores how mindfulness, deliberate engagement, and purposefulness that characterize the *slow* movement have long been vital elements in Indigenous ways of learning and knowing. We want to draw attention to the importance of holistic thinking and build on the values of Respect, Relevance, Reciprocity, and Responsibility (Kirkness & Barnhart, 1991), that underlie Indigenous pedagogies. Knowing that is informed by Slow and Indigenous ways can provide a roadmap, of sorts, to help us to navigate this shifting territory.

Over the past few years, we have worked together in teacher education and on various academic endeavours. We have come to this book as a culmination of our creative and academic work as sister scholars. Lorrie is a settler scholar and the birth mother of four children, two of whom have Cree heritage (Pukatawagan, Manitoba), and the grandmother of one granddaughter. Her two children with Cree heritage are from the first generation *not* to have been sent to residential schools. The Indigenous heritage of her two adult children and her granddaughter brings home, authentically, the importance of attuning to Indigenous ways and histories within curriculum and pedagogy. Lorrie's ancestry includes Scottish and Austrian-Romanian on her father's side, though both grandparents were themselves born in Moose Jaw, Saskatchewan. Her maternal ancestry includes Swedish, Norwegian, and Irish-Quebecois from Trois-Rivières. Family stories, connection to place, and distance in between have informed Lorrie's journey as a scholar, artist, educator, and mother. Shannon is a Member of the Métis Nation through her father, Edward Patrick Kane, whose grandmother, Mabel Monkman, was from St. Louis, Saskatchewan. On her mother's side, she is a second-generation Irish Canadian. She identifies as both Indigenous and white settler. As a scholar, this has informed her work in teacher education, where decolonizing teaching to make space for Indigenous pedagogies and voices is central to her work. Born on Treaty 6 territory and raised in Saskatoon by her mother, she has lived on Musqueam, Squamish, and Tsleil-Waututh territory since 1994 and is now a mother herself.

We are both from the prairies but are presently art educators who live and teach in Vancouver at the University of British Columbia. We feel and believe (these are different things) that these facts of our identities are pertinent to the work we are undertaking here, as you will see in the pages ahead. We invite you, dear reader, to place yourself as well within the text, to think about where you are now and from where you have come. How did your family come to be in the place they call home? On whose traditional territory do you live now? In other words: *What is your relationship to the place you live and the land on which you live?*

Before we move on, we'd like to add a note about terminology and identity in this book. We use the word Indigenous throughout this book because it refers not only to First Nations but also to Inuit, Métis, and non-Status folks. We have used the words white settler to describe ourselves deliberately, which is essential to our thinking in this book. Settler is a political word meant to evoke how most European-descended people came to live in Canada. It connects the process of colonization to the present and points to how many families continue to benefit from circumstances that arose during the earlier periods of colonization. Some of the objections to the word settler, however, are rooted in astute critiques from other Canadians, who, as people of colour, do not share the same dynastic relationship between the land and state. For example, the descendants of Black folks who escaped to Canada before and during the American Civil War, and the descendants of those from China who were brought here to build the railroad preceding confederation, did not benefit from many of the policies that were designed to draw immigrants from Europe. Neither have the many refugees from around the world who have arrived here more recently.

Nevertheless, our use of the word white does not dismiss the need for all Canadians, regardless of how or when they arrived, to engage in the work of decolonizing educational practices and curriculum. We also acknowledge that there are Indigenous people that object to the divisive potential of the word settler – it can evoke a lot of weight and guilt, but this is not our intention. We seek to keep relationships in mind throughout this text and be mindful of who we each are as readers and authors in relation to the ideas we raise. Again, tawâw – there is room for you here.

BRINGING INDIGENOUS KNOWLEDGE AND PEDAGOGIES INTO THE CLASS

For those of us brave enough to become teachers, the classroom is a zone of both enchantment and challenge. As teachers, we have many moments of loving our students, our colleagues, and our jobs.

However, if we are honest, we have occasional moments of significant struggle too. This is particularly true when the comfortable pattern of our days, units, or academic years are disrupted by forces beyond our control, placing demands upon us that can seem onerous and unreasonable. Sometimes, during curricular change, teachers feel entirely unprepared to implement new curricular requirements; this is exemplified by the challenge put to teachers today to enact the recommendations from the Truth and Reconciliation Commission (TRC, 2015c). Thus, there is anxiety felt today by many teachers in British Columbia and across the country, who are expected to include First Nations, Inuit, and Métis perspectives, knowledge, and pedagogies across the curriculum, and at every grade level, but often have no idea where to begin. This work can be challenging and sometimes uncomfortable. Still, we take heart in one of the Lil'wat Principles of Learning, that of Cwelelep, or "recognizing the need to sometimes be in a place of dissonance and uncertainty, to be open to new learning" (Sanford et al., 2012, p. 24). There is a lot to be learned when we lean into our discomfort.

Students in all teacher education programs across Canadian provinces receive some form of Indigenous education training as part of their overall professional and academic education. In some faculties, it comes in a required course, while other institutions blend content into pre-existing program structures. Whatever the case, Teacher Education programs in British Columbia are mandated by the BC Teacher's Council to provide teacher candidates with "at least three credit/ semester hours of study related to Indigenous Pedagogies and Unappropriated Indigenous knowledge and perspectives, and integration of these teachings throughout the program" (British Columbia Teachers' Council, 2023, p. 3). While this is more exposure to Indigenous content in education than many in-service teachers received during their teacher education or training, it no more prepares teacher candidates to grapple with the complexities of teaching Indigenous curriculum than any single course of instruction does in any other area.

Most teachers who received their Bachelor of Education before 2010, however, grew up with a dearth of learning about Indigenous peoples, cultures, and histories throughout both their K–12 and post-secondary education. At the start of every course she teaches, Shannon asks her students to reflect on what they recall learning about Indigenous people in their school experiences and where else they remember learning about Indigenous people. Their answers usually reflect that dearth quite clearly, except for the outliers who had relatively rich experiences. Once they reflect and account for why they know so little, students can better grapple with their anxiety, leaving them more open to learning. It is essential to think about why we do not know – at the heart of the answer is that we are *all* colonized peoples.

Teacher candidates (also known as student-teachers and pre-service teachers) report varying responses when they head into the schools for their practicum experiences. They may arrive at schools, brimming with new learning about Indigenous peoples and pedagogies and excited to create lessons and learning units that showcase their new knowledge, only to be paired with a school associate (or sponsor teacher) who does not share their enthusiasm, the impact of which can be rough. Similarly, a school associate may be excited to host a teacher candidate, knowing of the course in Indigenous education they have taken, and hoping to learn from their student-teacher and build their practice, only to discover that the person they were matched with was disinterested in the subject, or is fearful of the potential for negative consequences when including Indigenous content. A myriad of other possible combinations of factors exists, of course, but in the end, the results of such mismatching can be the same – disappointment and the continuation of avoidance or problematic practice.

For teacher candidates, we know that time and practice will fertilize their learning on Indigenous education, allowing it to blossom into the branches of their work with students. This does not happen without stops, starts, and uncertainties. After all, teaching is a messy business, but at least they have been introduced to the concepts, resources, and pedagogical strategies that can carry them forward. They will continue to need, however, good support and strong relationships. Their seasoned counterparts face different challenges to integrating this complex new content into their entire school days. We need to keep in mind that a single teacher works with anywhere between 15 and 210 students during a week, depending on whether they teach in an elementary or a high school. They may also have extracurricular duties within the school, committee work, staff obligations, and parent meetings, their own family and community responsibilities notwithstanding. Often, there is little energy left to pursue special topics and develop curricular materials and a body of resources to deploy them.

Our goal here is to provide a guide to basics about Indigenous education that will support both pre-service and in-service teachers at various career stages as they hone their practices. We have framed this goal as the acquisition of decolonial literacy, learning to revisit old frames of reference, to see how the colonization machine has informed provincial curricula, and to become more precise about what it means to engage in Indigenous education. First, we will set out some of the groundwork we have done to inform our later chapters.

INDIGENOUS WAYS AND RECONCILIATION

Viewing Indigenous content as *additional* deprives our students of the powerful benefits of infusing Indigenous voices, content, and pedagogies throughout the curriculum. Indigenous ways of knowing are inherently interdisciplinary, connected to lives lived in the real world, forming the epistemological threads that constitute our ways of being in the world. We agree with Goulet and Goulet (2014) that "the education of Indigenous children, and indeed all children, requires a more comprehensive view of life in its totality" (p. 25). With some cautions for non-Indigenous educators, Sandra Stein (2020) articulates a view of what it might mean to approach Indigenous content as a practice of infusion, in which Indigenous knowledges "become seamlessly infused in every aspect of the classroom, pedagogical content, and practices, so that the whole system takes on the flavour, if you will, of Indigenous knowledges" (p. 48).

Slow pedagogy, which is not to be confused with returning to all things analogue, nor simply taking more time, also presents *ways* of doing things that are more epistemological than curricular. We see a natural fit between Indigenous and Slow pedagogies as *ways* of being in the world, in which attending to teaching and learning is like the warp and the weft of the same cloth. Through Slow ways, we can challenge colonizing notions of time and reconnect with our embodied selves. "We need to embody different notions of time to access alternate sources of knowledge, including embodied ways of knowing" (Shahjahan, 2015, p. 499). It is a paradigm shift – a loosening of the stranglehold notions that modernity, technological advancement, and progress have wrought. We aim to take what at first blush may seem complex and perhaps overwhelming, bring it into practice, and demonstrate that Indigenous and Slow ways (storytelling, map-making, poetry, and visual art, traditional craft), can be integrated into a lived pedagogy, one with hope, intention, humility, and vision.

Lil'wat educator Lorna Williams worked with Kathy Sanford (2012) to imagine how teacher education could be decolonized by looking at some of the key principles of Indigenous education from the Lil'wat perspective. In their work, they make clear how Indigenous ways of knowing are centred on the agency and abilities of the students as compared with Western teacher-centric approaches. They offer six principles of Indigenous learning that are relational, such a "Kamúcwkalha … acknowledging the felt energy indicating group attunement and the emergence of a common group purpose" (p. 23), "Celhcelh … each person being responsible for their own and others learning, always seeking learning opportunities" (p. 23), and "A7xekcal … valuing our own expertise and considering how it helps the entire community beyond ourselves" (pp. 23–4). We have found each of these helpful considerations in thinking about how to weave our two perspectives together. As art teachers, we are well familiar with the energy that comes together when students work with their hands to produce something. We know that each person brings their talent to their work and that moments of frustration often precede breakthroughs in the process. We hope to make this clear in multiple curricular contexts throughout this book and show that when we relinquish colonial curriculum and pedagogies in cross-curricular contexts, we make space for all of our students to learn and grow in their ways.

We, collectively, have inherited our current colonial situation. In this era of time famine, tech pervasion, and climate change, people seem to be overwhelmed with "information" with never enough time to do anything about any of it. We turn to our preceding scholars (hooks, 2003; Freire, 1994) in leaning upon their notions of a *pedagogy of hope*. At this time, students at the elementary, secondary, and university levels report high rates of anxiety, depression, and hopelessness and claim that they simply cannot keep up with the demands placed on them from school, society, and social media. Students are not alone. Their elder generations suffer from work burnout and tech-overload, as they struggle with the time = money paradigm (BC Hydro, 2018; Berg & Seeber, 2017; Menzies, 2005; Menzies & Newson, 2007; Ylijoki & Mäntylä, 2003). Many, both old and young, are seeking ways to cope with this systemic emphasis on speed and productivity. The popularity of yoga, mindfulness, and slow food (amongst other things) is indicative of such a need. It may also account for the sudden revival of homemade bread that characterized the early days of the pandemic in 2020.

Simultaneously, we are experiencing an awakening to Indigenous peoples' concerns, rights, and pedagogies (Battiste, 2000; Deer, 2019; Dion, 2009; Donald, 2009, 2019; Restoule & Nardozzi, 2019). Here in Canada, there is no question that the last several years have brought significant positive change to Indigenous education at both K–12 and post-secondary institutions. Decades of Indigenous activism have culminated in the production and ratification of several important documents, including the *United Nations Declaration on the Rights of Indigenous Peoples* (UNDRIP, 2009) and the Association of Canadian Deans of Education's (ACDE) *Accord on in Indigenous Education* (2010). Each of these has produced bold statements that support self-determination, reconciliation, and decolonizing education. For example, Article 15 of UNDRIP states that the diversity of Indigenous peoples should be reflected in public education. Indeed, the ACDE Accord includes in its intended goals that a commitment to Indigenous education be fostered within teacher candidates by creating immersive experiences that connect them to Indigenous learning contexts and to "explore and question their own sense of power and privilege (or lack thereof) within Canadian society as compared with others in that society" (ACDE, 2010). Further, the TRC (2015c) released the *Calls to Action* aimed at education, requiring provincial governments to fund teacher education programs in ways that specifically respond to those goals (p. 7, no. 62, ii). The mandate is clear, and the path is set, but sometimes the going is sluggish.

While these calls to action and principles laid out a promising direction for development and growth, practitioners in the field seem to lag in actualizing them. In 2015, the Canadian Teachers Federation (CTF) undertook a study of their membership's perspectives on Aboriginal education in public schools in Canada. The resulting thirty-four–page document, published online, shows that 51% of surveyed teachers occasionally teach Aboriginal content and perspectives, 41% feel that Aboriginal issues are somewhat represented in their school curriculum, and only 17% of teachers feel very confident with their knowledge of Aboriginal content and perspectives (CTF, 2015). While such a survey considers recently minted teachers who have taken required courses in Indigenous education and those who are seasoned teachers, when asked if they had ever participated in Aboriginal professional development, only 52% said yes. We are not as far along in honouring the UNDRIP and ACDE Accord mandates, much less the spirit of Indigenous education and the energies of Indigenous faculty, as it might be hoped.

To be clear, we are not suggesting that the distance between the goals stated by UNDRIP and ACDE and reality is the fault of an apathetic body of teacher practitioners. Instead, we lay this difficulty squarely at the feet of colonialism, which has quietly honed and shaped our general ideas about learners and learning, specifically about Indigenous learners and learning, from the beginning. Teachers, and those coming into teacher education programs, feel ill-prepared to grapple with Indigenous education because they *were* ill-prepared (Dion, 2009). Many teachers struggle with the seeming foreignness (ironically) of Indigenous pedagogy because they are unsure of what it means. Further, they are uncertain of what it will mean to them to learn about it. Many have adopted what Susan Dion (2009) terms perfect stranger positioning, unaware of their un-knowing.

For Indigenous students and teachers, the impact of colonial thinking in schools is even more deeply felt. In addition to the resonance of residential school trauma through multiple generations, colonial curricula have also had significant cultural impacts in the imposition of what Battiste (2013) has termed cognitive imperialism, or "whitewashing the mind as a result of forced assimilation, English education, Eurocentric humanities and sciences, and living in Eurocentric context complete with media, books, laws and values" (p. 26). While there has been a plethora of Indigenous educators and authors producing multiple and multimodal resources to turn the tide on this problem in recent years, there are still many educators who have not taken the time to immerse themselves in these resources. This can cause a lot of discomfort and emotional labour for Indigenous students in classroom contexts. Sheila Cote-Meek (2015) has written extensively on this subject, detailing student accounts of hearing misinformation about Indigenous peoples from non-Indigenous instructors or being called upon in classes to act as an informant on Indigenous realities. She reminds us that as teachers, we must "consider who the subjects are in the classroom and how they receive [Indigenous] content … [and] … understand how the subject positions of the student and the educator delivering the historical testimony may affect the dynamics that emerge at the site" (p. 33). This resonates with Huia Tomlins-Jahnke's (2019) questions regarding classroom dynamics where Indigenous students are concerned when she states: "who gets to be ignorant and uphold the privilege of not knowing are those who not only have the luxury of ignorance but hold the power to be ignorant" (p. 89). To do this work, we need to be humble and allow ourselves to be disempowered as we unlearn old ways of being. This is the work of decolonization.

In order to truly prepare in-service and pre-service teachers to undertake this work in meaningful ways, the process of decolonization has to be enacted and embodied in our courses. That is, we must peel back the layers of colonial messaging received through decades of curricular content that either wholly excluded or misrepresented Indigenous peoples, often locking them into a historic past designed to render them non-entities in the present (Dion, 2009). Transforming colonial perspectives into more holistic ones better suited to the meaningful consideration of what it means to engage in Indigenous education takes time. Despite the implementation of teacher education courses designed to do this work, in practice, adequate time to enact the transformative learning required to do it well is not often available. This speaks to one of the major pitfalls of privileging clock time over seasonal and cyclical time. This approach does not allow for things to take as long as they take – it is the genesis of our constantly rushed pace. And when we rush, important things get left behind.

We recognize that this process may come to some more easily than others, and that we all begin our journey into Indigenous education at different starting points. So, throughout our text, we have woven together our two key pedagogical approaches, Indigenous and Slow, and have expanded our weaving metaphor where possible to illustrate the many connections and abundant possibilities taking these two approaches together can hold.

THE MEDICINE WHEEL FRAMEWORK, OUR LOOM

To weave a cloth, one works the weft threads over the warp threads that are fastened to the sturdy framework of the loom. As we weave our thoughts and ideas of Indigenous and Slow pedagogies, we have turned to support our cloth on the organizing framework of the Medicine Wheel, and so, it is in this way our loom.

The Medicine Wheel, or Sacred Circle, has been used by many (but certainly not all) Indigenous peoples across Turtle Island for millennia, particularly in the Great Plains region. More than seventy stone wheels can still be found throughout the Canadian prairies, laid out in the grasses, artifacts of long-ago lessons. In Saskatchewan, where we each (Shannon and Lorrie) grew up, the Medicine Wheel was ubiquitous, if not in school, then in the community. Shannon was introduced to Medicine Wheel teachings during her undergraduate years at the University of Saskatchewan through friends in what was then called Native Studies and through Indigenous artists she met and worked with in visual art, and art history classes and teachings sometimes offered at powwows and feasts. As a scholar, she has spent a lot of time researching how teachers and academics have put this framework to use in their classrooms and regularly uses the Medicine Wheel when planning courses. In addition to offering a wholistic framework of selfhood, the wheel also points to seasonal and cyclical understandings of time (Cajete, 2004; Fixico, 2003).

Lorrie's connection with the Medicine Wheel began when she accepted her first teaching position in the Cree community school in Pukatawagan, Manitoba. As the art specialist teacher for the school of four hundred students, she felt it necessary as a new teacher to not import Western art methods and examples. She turned to local and regional artists for examples and inspiration. This initiation into Indigenous culture stretched well beyond those foundational years of teaching in the North and further connected her to community and teachings when she moved to Vancouver to pursue graduate studies with her young family. Her initial research study focused on Indigenous women artists' learning experiences. This early research opened her eyes to the importance of lived-learning, collaborative teaching and learning, and a holistic approach to both teaching and scholarly engagement. It was also during this time she first learned about residential schools and the negative impacts on many students and communities. All of this is to say that scholarly, personal, and spiritual exploration and growth has brought her to a place of deep appreciation of the wisdom that is represented within the teachings of the Medicine Wheel.

The Medicine Wheel, our loom as it were, forms the structure of the weaving of ideas we will do in this book. Especially because the internet is full of Cree, Anishinaabe, and New Age versions of Medicine Wheels, we wanted our readers to be able to access this important reference as well. So, we have chosen to rely on the wheels found in *The Sacred Tree*, written collaboratively and published in 1984 by Phil Lane Jr. (Dakota and Chickasaw), Judie Bopp, Michael Bopp, and Lee Brown (Cherokee). In the years leading up to its publication, it was developed as a project of the Four Worlds International Development organization. Created in consultation with a wide array of Elders and Knowledge Keepers from all around Turtle Island, the book contains a wealth of kind and good-hearted teachings to help each of us be in the world in a good way. They share the teachings of the wheel moving clockwise, beginning in the East, where the sun rises, and we start our journey as infants. This quadrant is coloured yellow and asks us to consider ourselves as spiritual beings, offering us guidance on how to begin and proceed with our journey. In the South, symbolized by the colour red, they offer consideration of what it means to be emotional beings as we explore the power and potential of our youth. In the West, we are asked to understand ourselves more fully as physical beings. The colour black also ties us to the physicality of the land and encourages a more mature consideration of ourselves in relation to the land and other physical beings. Finally, in the white quadrant of the North, we focus on ourselves as intellectual beings as we consider the lessons we have learned on our journey. "The Medicine Wheel is a symbolic tool that helps us to see the interconnectedness of our being with the rest of creation" (Lane et al., 1984, p. 41). Immediately, we see a deep resonance with the tenets of Slow.

The conventional Medicine Wheel, with its four directions and colours, forms a standard x/y axis. In our work, though, we also include the z-axis to create a sphere to indicate both the element of time and a spiritual connectedness and wholeness within a third and fourth dimension. We also ascribe Dr. Verna Kirkness's 4Rs of

Indigenous Education (Kirkness & Barnhardt, 1991) to each quadrant, placing Respect in the East, Relevance in the South, Reciprocity in the West, and Responsibility in the North. This is not a fixed thing but an ongoing collaboration and negotiation. Even in the crafting of this text, we took our work to our peers, a community of teacher educators, senior scholars, Elders, and students with whom we work, to workshop it, recognizing it is a living document, even once in print. The point is less about the accuracy of where we place these various attributes and more about making space for ambiguity in our learning.

WARP AND WEFT: CONNECTING SLOW TO INDIGENOUS WAYS

We are collectively suffering from the freneticism of our *fast-paced* society, which feeds the chronic anxiety of time famine. While the slow living movement, led by Italian Carlo Petrini's *Slow Food* in 1986, paved the way for a return to slowness in a number of fields, since that time, our lives beyond food have sped up with the development of instant messaging, high-speed internet, and a thousand "time-saving" gadgets (Petrini et al., 2007). Our lives are regulated according to clock-time, rather than lived, fluid time. We are, as Hannah Arendt (1958) predicted, conditioned by our production of things. Shahjahan (2015) tells us that we've been living in a colonized time and way that separates us from our embodied selves, privileging our minds over all other forms of knowing and being. Menzies and Newson (2007) seem to agree when they warn that without natural life rhythms, "there is a danger that the sense of rootedness in anything embodied and physical will become that much weaker. Accordingly, the social habits, the temporal practices and social rhythms associated with embodied reflection, memory and dialogue may wither as well" (p. 94).

This concept of time mirrors Indigenous ways of knowing. Time is cyclical, flowing like a river through seasonal changes that repeat year after year (Fixico, 2003). Observing the way things work together across seasonal cycles is the foundation of Indigenous knowledges. In discussing Indigenous science, Cajete (2004) describes it as a process which "strives to understand and apply the knowledge gained from participation in the here and now, and emphasize our role as one of nature's members rather than as striving to be in control of it" (p. 47). In this way of thinking, time is not a jailor but a teacher. Things take as long as they take and happen when they do. Grasses and berries don't keep calendars, but they know when to ripen based on their experience of the contexts in which they grow. Bison and caribou keep only to the schedule of food availability and safety. We humans used to be much more the same.

As educators, we see the call to slowness as an invitation to more purposeful actions – mindfulness, deliberate engagement, and deep inquiry. This can move us back to asking questions of *why* rather than simply *how*. It also encourages integral care about our actions and the implications of such actions on others and the world. Slow reading, for example, as advocated by Sven Birkerts (1994), invites the reader to delve into and contemplate a text deeply, now a rare act in a world overwhelmed with the instantaneousness of tweets, online reading, memes, and sidebar notifications, constantly asking us to click through the text and away from the central message. When engaging with a particularly challenging text, a deep read is required. We are referring to the emotionally heavy material that requires sensitive and authentic engagement, such as texts that can lead us to understand the work of reconciliation. We see parallels here between slow reading and Indigenous storywork (Archibald, 2008), where attentive listening and recursive experiences of stories allow meaning and understanding to build over time. While instantaneous learning can also occur in these contexts, it is not an expectation, and such insights might be viewed as gifts.

Recently, several documents and books have been generated in British Columbia that reflect both generalized and culturally specific principles of Indigenous education. The First People's Principles of Learning, developed by the First Nations Education Steering Committee (FNESC) in 2008, is perhaps the best-known example. Its nine principles are frequently used in teacher preparation programs and by school districts as a way of providing an avenue into practices in Indigenous education. Several more examples have recently come out as well, such as the previously mentioned Lil'wat Principles, developed by Lorna Williams (Sanford et al., 2012), and the Ska'ada principles, developed by Sara Davidson, in conjunction with her father, Haida artist Robert Davidson (Davidson & Davidson, 2018). Each of these approaches is rooted in the ontology of interconnectedness and relationships. Unlike the common focus in colonial classroom contexts on production, each of these sets of principles places much more emphasis on process and experience. They invert the banking model of education (Freire, 1970) of teacher-knowledge producing student understanding in favour of a view that centres the process of student learning facilitated by teacher knowledge (also, Ingold, 2017). But while these old ideas have been made newly available to educators, there remains a great deal of trepidation on how to enact them, how to address and include Indigenous content, and even what role non-Indigenous teachers should have in this work in the first place. Exacerbating efforts to engage in Indigenous education in meaningful ways is the very same time starvation to which we have earlier referred. Enter Slow pedagogy ...

We have identified central attributes to Slow, following an *exhausting* review of texts, articles, and manifestos (not claiming *exhaustive*, as this is impossible): Ayers et al. (2017); Berg and Seeber (2017); Goldschmidt et al. (2016); Holt (2002); Honoré (2004); Laufer (2011); Lewis (2004); Lipson (2012); Menzies (2005); Menzies and Newson (2007); Mikics (2013); Payne and Wattchow (2009); Shahjahan (2015); Shaw et al. (2013); Thiessen (2017); Thom (2019); Wellesley-Smith (2015); Ylijoki and Mäntylä (2003). In chapter 3, Slow and Indigenous Ways, we more fully explore the relationship between the Slow (everything) movement and Indigenous pedagogies and ways as expressed in the literature. In the meantime, we have identified the following themes that could be used to describe the tenets of Slow. In all of the literature, there are many overlapping ideas amongst all the above authors, with some specifically identified below. There are two overarching governing features to these tenets:

1) A deep ethic of care – including sustainability (Ayers et al., 2017; Berg & Seeber, 2017; Holt, 2002; Menzies & Newson, 2007; Ylijoki & Mäntylä, 2003),
2) A naturally paced experience that is not clock-timed, but where one takes the time to explore and allow for serendipity (Ayers et al., 2017; Berg & Seeber 2017; Holt, 2002; Lipson, 2012, Thiessen, 2017).

And four tenets of Slow:

- lived and experiential (physical self) (Berg & Seeber, 2017; Holt, 2002; Honoré, 2004, Lipson, 2012; Payne & Wattchow, 2009; Shaw et al., 2013; Wellesley-Smith, 2015),
- place-conscious – a deep connection to where and when you are (Holt, 2002; Lipson, 2012; Shahjahan, 2015),
- relational, social connectedness, cultural, learning from other, teaching and sharing with others (Lipson, 2012; Menzies & Newson, 2007, Wellesley-Smith, 2015; Ylijoki & Mäntylä, 2003),
- connecting to one's inner-self (emotional, spiritual, soulful; Nakamura & Csikszentmihalyi, 2014; Shahjahan, 2015).

The overarching principles are evident in all of the sub-tenets, so they were not independent tenets but rather co-dependent. For instance, a *deep ethic of care* connects to the tenet *relational and social connectedness* and likewise, with place consciousness and each of the other tenets. These concepts are not just threads lying one beside the next but really woven and then felted together so that they become inextricably entwined and mutually supportive.

Here, we reimagine education and question how current modalities are meeting the stated intentions of provincial and educational actors to support the emotional connection to learners and learning for which the inclusion of Indigenous content calls. In British Columbia, the urgency of this work has come further to the fore with the addition of Standard 9 to the *Professional Standards for BC Educators*, which states: "Educators respect and value the history of First Nations, Inuit and Métis in Canada and the impact of the past on the present and the future. Educators contribute towards truth, reconciliation, and healing. Educators foster a deeper understanding of ways of knowing and being, histories, and cultures of First Nations, Inuit, and Métis" (British Columbia Teachers' Council, 2019, p. 5). The implication is that this work is no longer optional.

In this era of opinion over reason, of *alternate facts*, how do we nurture teachers who are thoughtful in both depth and breadth, sensitive to the complexities of identity, and who know the difference between fabrication and fact? How might we embrace First Peoples Principles of Learning (FNESC, 2008) to inform our teacher preparation practice?

What might it mean to develop a decolonial literacy that will support Indigenous and non-Indigenous students in making connections to learning and meaning in their lives? We seek to answer some of these questions in ways that will honour and respond to Indigenous pedagogies and invite dialogue that will build the massive social change this educational problem requires.

While we are aware of current academic work that focuses on the importance of returning to slowness, of the negative impacts of speed in the academy, and of scholarly work that focuses on Indigenous pedagogy and ways of knowing, we are not aware of any text that attempts to weave both together in an extended and explicit way. By uniting these two seemingly disparate ways of looking at teaching, learning, and being, we will show how very similar they are. By doing so doing, we hope to build support for academics and non-Indigenous educators grappling with angst around the inclusion of Indigenous content. We also hope to support our Indigenous colleagues, who often report feelings of fatigue as they become the only go-to person in the schools and districts in which they work (Stein, 2020). We also see this book as being a potential resource for teacher educators who need ways to introduce this subject matter in their courses and to their colleagues grappling with discomfort as well. We also see this text as providing a roadmap to educators and teacher educators to return to questions of why, beyond how. Rather than crafting yet another competing paradigmatic model, we synthesize those previously proposed into a meta-model so that the harmonious qualities among them may be made visible, embraceable, and useable.

Medicine Wheel teachings are used by many Indigenous peoples as guides to live in good relationships and expressing ways of being in this world that honour the holistic nature of our collective being; this is a framework. Its relationship to seasonal and cyclical time connects it directly to many of the considerations of slowness. We have also found weaving to be an apt metaphor, as we are both avid visual/ textile artists/artisans (figure 1.2).

We literally and figuratively weave together; our fabric is both physical and metaphorical, as we work our ideas and teachings into a whole cloth. This book is one of many written works we have crafted together. One of our favourite textile artifacts is a cloth that we wove

Figure 1.2. Shannon holding one of the prototype shawls produced collaboratively in Lorrie's textiles classroom.

Source: Courtesy of Lorrie Miller.

and then felted together. For us, this is a powerful metaphor as the act of weaving makes a fabric stronger than any single strand. Much as the warm water motion of the felting process creates a significantly stronger, sturdier, and warmer fabric by drawing the warp and weft more tightly together, we see our weaving of Slow and Indigenous pedagogies in the same way. We are stronger together.

2

Building Decolonial Literacy for Indigenous Education

Leddy: Years ago, just before she left Saskatchewan to move to Vancouver Island, my mother spent several summers developing and nurturing a lovely English-style garden in the backyard of our prairie family home. She grew Maltese Cross, Delphiniums, Columbines, Heliopsis, Lythrum, and Baby's Breath. With plenty of sunlight and careful watering, the wealth of foliage yielded several boast-worthy bouquets each year without leaving the garden bare. Creating that space also meant many happy hours of browsing at garden centres, learning Latin names for things, and quiet, meditative periods of early evening hand watering. It was truly a lovely thing.

Although I have begun and nurtured several small gardens during my years in Vancouver, it was only once I moved to my previous home that I began to think of planning such a garden of my own. I had access to a wee postage stamp of a yard, with a few areas of full sun and lots of areas of dappled or full shade. I consulted with Mom about what plants would be best and what might work well. She even gifted me some Daylily, Crocosmia, and Daisy plants from her own garden to get me going. I brought bag after bag of soil and fertilizer home to enrich my garden beds, watered the plants almost nightly by hand, and daydreamed about how lush and colourful my little garden would be in years in the years to come.

After eight years of tomatoes with blossom end rot (despite vast quantities of lime and bone meal added to the soil), daylilies that sprouted annually but never got as far as producing flowers, and daisies that refused to come up again after only two years, I was finally begin-ning to feel defeated. Only the crocosmia had survived over all that time, along with a lilac bush and a few scraggly peonies. I was able to sustain my collection of potted annuals and always had a lovely spray of potted begonias and fuchsias nestled into an old wagon in a shady part of the yard, but all of my other efforts seem to come to naught.

The garden was overhung by a twenty-year-old sugar pine, whose roots always made soil turning and planting a challenge, notwithstanding its significant contributions to the acidity of the soil. When we moved in, there were already a few hostas in the ground, along with some very twiggy shrubbery. As I planned my return to the garden one fall evening, after several summers of being distracted by studying and teaching, it suddenly occurred to me that I had been thinking like a colonizer. I wanted to impose my vision of the ideal garden onto a place that I had never taken the time to understand. I was ignoring material reality in favour of my own ambi-tions. I was really working against my garden rather than with it.

Building on that flash of insight, I began to let go of how I wanted things to be and paid attention to how they were. I began to peel away my prescriptive ideas of what the garden should be and observed more thoughtfully what was working in my garden. With my imagination freed from the bounds of its previously limited vision, I began to see new possibilities. I planted salal, a few ferns, and another hosta. I planted a currant bush in the space where the tomatoes never really grew. Although I only enjoyed my new, more naturalized garden for a few years, it was already clear what a difference a change in my thinking made, and I can now see that the garden was already lovely in a way I never appreciated before. This spring, I will plant a garden in my new home, attending to all of the lessons learned from the last one.

Thomas King (2012) has written extensively on the impacts of colo-nization on Indigenous peoples in both the United States and Canada in his book *The Inconvenient Indian*. With humour and grace, he cites the events, people, and legislation that have shaped Turtle Island in an unflinching account of how it all went down … through Indigenous eyes. Before him, Vine Deloria Jr. (1969) offers an accounting of colo-nial impact as well in *Custer Died for Your Sins*. Their work draws to the fore the importance of recognizing that these accounts stand out because Indigenous perspectives have been suppressed from curricula

WE ARE ALL RELATED.

Figure 2.1. *We Are All Related*, 2018.

Source: Courtesy of Shannon Leddy.

and hidden from public reckoning. Paulette Reagan (2010) has written extensively on *how* these erasures have informed our thinking *about* and relations *with* Indigenous peoples in her examination of what is truly required to affect reconciliation. In her book, *Unsettling the Settler Within*, Reagan suggests that we must each undergo a process of decolonization; that is, letting go of what we think we know about Indigenous peoples long enough to discover *why* we think as we do. The goal is to come to a place collectively where we might consider how we can do better. Marie Battiste (2000, 2013), Susan Dion (2007), and Verna St. Denis and Carol Schick (2003; Schick & St. Denis, 2005), and all write about how a colonized view of Indigenous peoples, and of education itself, has kept a status quo in place that, historically, manifests in teachers' and student teachers' indifference to Indigenous peoples and their contemporary struggles for justice and recognition, and refusal to relearn about them. Sheila Cote-Meek (2015) has also written about the impacts of colonized thinking on Indigenous students in post-secondary institutions as they experience microaggressions, racisms, and misinformation about themselves and their Nations daily in university courses from both fellow students and instructors.

In the context of Indigenous education, the concept of ontology is important as we consider what we have learned about Canada, whom we believe ourselves to be as Canadians, and what we believe about other Canadians and our collective history. We live here on this land and in this time. In these ways, and many others, we are all related (figure 2.1). This artwork of a medicine wheel and sweetgrass shows a mix of hues that overlap, contrast, divide, balance, and complement one another, much like we Canadians do. Many of us fondly carry the belief that Canada is a wonderful country, known for engaging in international peacekeeping, maintaining a fair justice system, having a strong social safety net, and comfort foods such as butter tarts and poutine. And we are not entirely wrong in that belief. We have our rough edges and our disagreements, but overall, we are lacking in the dictatorships, capital punishments, famines, military coups, and kangaroo courts endured by some of our fellow humans. But the idea of *Canada-The-Good* that has been historically nurtured in classrooms, kitchens, barns, and garages across the county has been shattered recently as darker aspects of our nation's past have come to light through the TRC (2015a, 2015b) and the 2021 discovery of 215 unmarked graves at the Kamloops IRS site (and repeated at multiple sites across the country);

the Inquiry into Missing and Murdered Indigenous Women and Girls (MMIWG); conflicts over territorial sovereignty between First Nations and industrialists; and the torturously difficult relationship between provincial child welfare systems and Indigenous peoples that have necessitated legislation such as Jordan's Principle (Canada, House of Commons, 2007), so that Indigenous children in Canada could be guaranteed equitable access to the same government-funded services as non-Indigenous children. The fight for Indigenous recognition, equity, and justice definitely feels Sisyphean at times.

HISTORICALLY ROOTED THOUGHT: WE ARE ALL COLONIZED PEOPLE

So, where did this tendency to historicize or avoid Indigenous peoples in the curriculum originate? On what is our collective confirmation bias built? There are two central concepts that have historically rooted our thinking in this way, whose tendrils still hamper new growth: *terra nullius* is the idea that the new world was a vast and unoccupied place, because since the native inhabitants were not Christian, they could not be human; and the Doctrine of Discovery, issued in 1493, laid out the framework for colonization based on the assertion of terra nullius. In America, these notions formed the backbone of Manifest Destiny, the mid-nineteenth century idea that it was the God-given right and responsibility of citizens of the United States to expand westward and continue to claim and develop lands stretching across the entire continent (King, 2012). While this thinking was not explicitly taken up in Canada and given a tidy title, certainly the thrust of colonial enterprise into nearly every corner of the northern part of the continent seems to indicate that a similar spirit was alive here as well. It is important to keep in mind that the Canadian amalgamation was in part a response to the pressure from our southern neighbours, as the American dream to thrust out on all the lands within their reach was a real threat to Canada's own expansion plans. The porousness of the newly imagined border meant that the ideas of "free" land and land lotteries for settlers linked to the *manifest* thinking of our southern cousins.

In light of several contemporary and ongoing conflicts between Indigenous peoples and industrial expansion, we continue to see the resonance of colonial thinking at work. For example, the Oka Resistance of 1990 fuelled a stand-off between Mohawk people and the residents of the town of Oka, Quebec, when the Oka Golf Club applied to expand their course onto lands that contained the Pine Hill Cemetery where many Mohawk ancestors were buried. More recently, the 2016–17 American protest of the Standing Rock Sioux against the Dakota Access Pipeline featured the bulldozing of sacred burial grounds, the use of attack dogs, and military forces using water cannons on protesters in sub-zero weather. Their rationale for such grave abuses? They had the right. Similarly, in Canada, the Unist'ot'en Camp protested against the incursion of the Coastal GasLink Pipeline on Wet'suwet'en territory. Given that for the most part, British Columbia is untreatied, and therefore unceded territory, ongoing discussions, both within government and industry around who has the right it is to decide the uses of their lands, are somewhat mystifying from the perspective of those who live with, rather than on, the land. It should be noted that both within the Wet'suwet'en and Standing Rock Sioux Nations, there are those who support industry and see both pipelines as a potential source of economic growth for their Nations, which should be taken as evidence that Indigenous peoples are not a monolith and, in many ways, share the concerns of their fellow North Americans. But in returning to the philosophical underpinnings that make such protests necessary, their origin is certainly connected to the key concepts in this section.

The legacy of terra nullius and the Doctrine of Discovery (Calderon, 2014; Seawright, 2014) remains resonant and pervasive, leaving ample evidence for scholars to take up and interrogate. But it is not just through the practice of delivering education within K–12 classrooms and the halls of academe that the story of colonization, and its erroneous underpinnings, continues to cement itself into our collective national psyche. Rather, sites of informal learning and the attrition achieved through colonial policy have also had contributions to make. In the following sections, we offer four key ideas to work through as you begin to develop your decolonial lexicon: ontology, identity, place, and relationships. But first, let's talk about what we mean when we say *decolonial literacy*.

IT IS *NOT* ABOUT THE LESSON PLANS

When confronted with darker aspects of Canadian history, many people first experience shock, grief, and even shame as they come to grips with the legacy of colonization – discomfort is necessary to the process of learning to decolonize. While some are spurred on to action by their learning, others retreat and avoid this difficult knowledge. Still, others opt for outright denial. These reactions might be considered as aspects of what Susan Dion (2007) refers to as "perfect stranger" positioning (p. 179), formulated through what we "know, what [we] do not know and what [we] refuse to know" (p. 331) about Indigenous peoples. In many ways, being a perfect stranger indicates a successful result for colonial conditioning. For many years, curricula across Canada, where it bothered to include Indigenous peoples at all, was a grand exercise in confirmation bias. By locating Indigenous people solidly in the past and treating them as a small bump in the development of Canada (Battiste, 2000; Dion, 2009), or by ignoring our contributions to the collective past entirely, it became possible for Canadians *not* to know Indigenous peoples as peers in the present, or to know them only as the stereotypes and caricatures spread by media and casual conversation. More than once, I have been in an elementary school classroom in which some child innocently asserts that there are no Indians left in Canada. (To be clear, we are in no way suggesting that every Canadian occupies the position of a *perfect stranger*. In fact, many non-Indigenous teachers have strong and positive relations with Indigenous peoples and communities. But those are not the folks who are struggling to include Indigenous concepts and content in their work with students.)

Decolonizing is a complex word that can provoke a variety of responses. Eve Tuck and K. Wayne Yang (2012) provide an extensive discussion of why decolonization should not be subsumed within broader social justice discourses because so doing is reductive of the long-rooted injustices that colonization has wrought on Indigenous peoples. They suggest instead adopting an "ethic of incommensurability" (p. 1) as a way to unsettle innocence, to maintain focus on Indigenous futurisms, and to move the project of decolonization away from the realm of metaphor and into the realm of action (p. 28). They want the word to be understood literally, calling for recognition of the stark differences between the ways in which Indigenous peoples understand and relate to the land and the ways it has been perceived and understood by those more newly arrived. In the wake of this recognition, they further call for the repatriation of all land and the return of its stewardship to Indigenous peoples. That is, we recognize, a lot to swallow. But we would like to suggest that the reason this is hard to swallow is because we have been trained to think so. We offer in the following sections a few key concepts that we have found helpful in detecting and tracking how the legacy of colonization requires that we begin to decolonize, starting with our minds. By turning to Indigenous perspectives, as illustrated in figure 2.2, we can begin *doing* this important work and bring it into our praxis.

This is about finding ways into learning that connect with our humanity, ways that allow students to find and explore their gifts, and that endows each of us with the responsibility to seek sustainability and balance as we develop our collective future. This is a holistic view of teaching and learning, of education, and it begins with us as teachers. However, we know from hearing it repeatedly in teacher education classrooms that what teachers really want is the lesson plan – the readily deployable resource that makes it all safe and easy to do. If you find yourself anxious to flip through this book, looking for where the lesson plans are, you will be disappointed. When considering each of the following – Indigenous education, Indigenous pedagogy, Slow pedagogy – we know that for none of them, is it about the lesson plans. Rather, it is about recognizing the colonial systems we have inherited and the anti-Indigenous racism that informs them, then developing new understandings, resources, and pedagogies that help move both ourselves and our students into new ways of learning together. It is about accepting the ways in which the curriculum we grew up with has blinded us to Indigenous peoples, understanding the consequences of our cultured collective ignorance, and figuring out how to do better. Lesson plans are only useful for including Indigenous content and perspectives if we have done our own decolonizing work first. Otherwise, they become an additive "beads and feathers" approach, which is more or less how we came to be in this bind in the first place. But do not feel like this is something that all has to happen at once. Perhaps the kindest thing you can do for yourself and your students, Dear Reader, is to acknowledge that this is something that you are learning about as well – you don't need to know it all! You can be a *co-learner* with your students.

It is possible, in each territory across Canada, to find Elders, Wisdom Keepers, and (if we are lucky), also Education Advisory committees. In BC, for instance, there is FNESC, which is the First Nations Education Steering Committee. They have advised many educators, developed education programs and highly detailed and useful curriculum documents, and produced a poster version (see figure 2.3)

Characteristics of Aboriginal Worldviews and Perspectives

Community Involvement:
Process & Protocols

Emphasis
on Identity

The Power
of Story

Engagement with the
Land, Nature, the Outdoors

Traditional
Teaching

Local Focus

Language
and Culture

Awareness
of History

**Connectedness
and
Relationship**

Experiential
Learning

The Role of
the Teacher

Learning
Environment
and Resources

Community
Engagement

Flexibility
(scheduling, program/
course configuration,
grouping)

Teacher
Preparation

Leadership
and Staffing

A Positive,
Learner-Centred
Approach

**Attributes of
Responsive Schooling**

Themes that emerged from the gatherings serve as organizers for the insights and ideas presented in this document. This circle graphic represents them, showing how themes identified with respect to the attributes of responsive schooling address and complement the themes associated with characteristics of Aboriginal Worldviews and Perspectives.

Figure 2.2. Aboriginal world views.

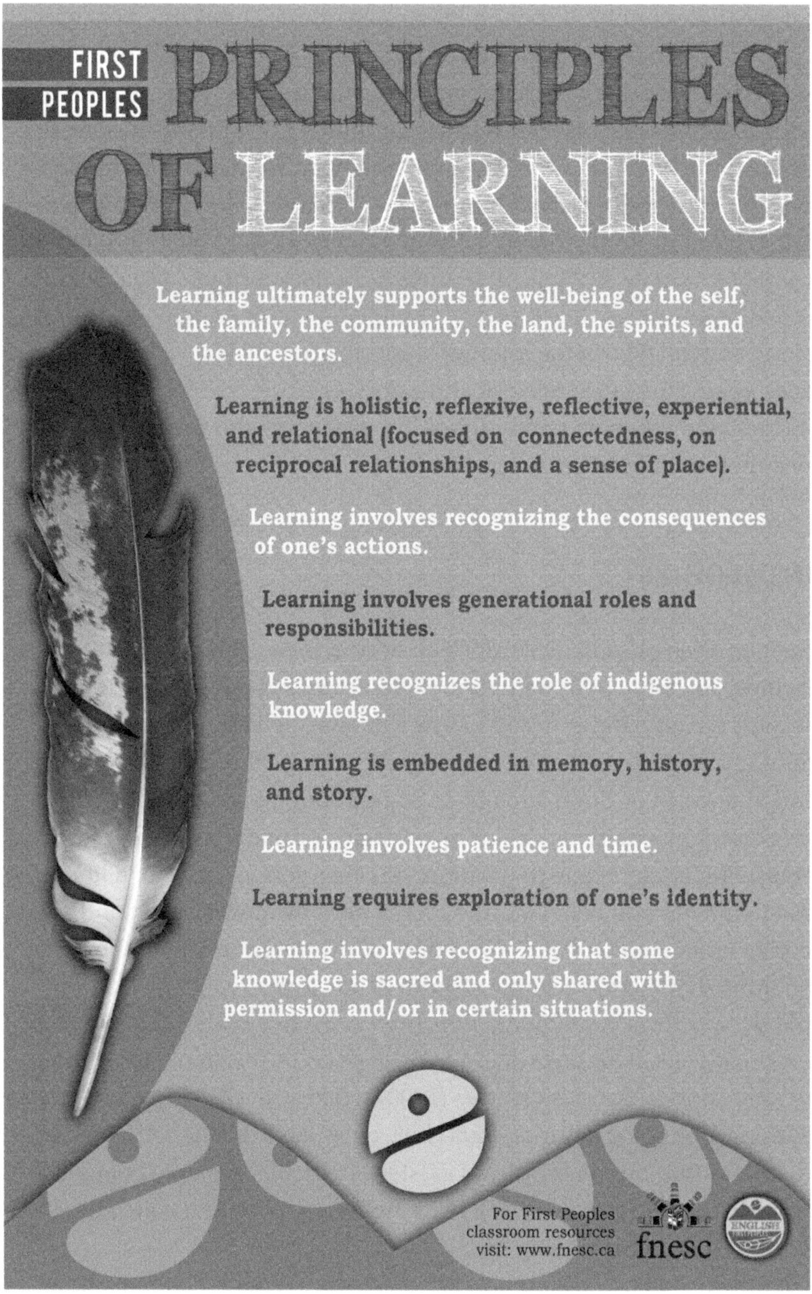

FIRST PEOPLES PRINCIPLES OF LEARNING

Learning ultimately supports the well-being of the self, the family, the community, the land, the spirits, and the ancestors.

Learning is holistic, reflexive, reflective, experiential, and relational (focused on connectedness, on reciprocal relationships, and a sense of place).

Learning involves recognizing the consequences of one's actions.

Learning involves generational roles and responsibilities.

Learning recognizes the role of indigenous knowledge.

Learning is embedded in memory, history, and story.

Learning involves patience and time.

Learning requires exploration of one's identity.

Learning involves recognizing that some knowledge is sacred and only shared with permission and/or in certain situations.

For First Peoples classroom resources visit: www.fnesc.ca **fnesc**

Figure 2.3. First Peoples Principles of Learning.

Sources: British Columbia (2015); FNESC (2008). Copyright © Province of British Columbia. All rights reserved. Reproduced with permission of the Province of British Columbia.

that has become ubiquitous in classrooms throughout the province. It is also possible to search a wide range of lesson and unit plans on the web developed by reliable and authentic sources, such as provincial Indigenous education advisory committees, Truth and Reconciliation Commission of Canada, and provincial teacher's federations. The University of British Columbia now has a website called Decolonizing Teaching Indigenizing Learning developed by Shannon and a group of graduate students that offers a compendium of valuable and authentic resources developed by Indigenous people. The wealth of resources available on the internet seems to grow by leaps and bounds every year! However, none of those lesson plans, we have come to realize, have any true value unless the teachers who use them have done their own decolonizing homework.

ONTOLOGIES

Teachers often grapple with much anxiety in their work: anxiety about teaching, anxiety about getting it right, anxiety about offending people, and anxiety about not being exactly sure what ontology means. Ontology is about the nature of being, the way we are, and the way we think the world is. From a religious standpoint, this relates to whether you believe in a deity or not, or in one deity, or many. From a political standpoint, it may relate to whether you are a conservative or a liberal based on what you believe is the role of both the government and the people. From a metaphysical standpoint, this might relate to whether you think that there is a single version of any given reality or that multiple perspectives confabulate to form a collective reality that we can never really get at because of our insistence on the myth of individuality. Philosopher Jean-Luc Nancy (2000) tells us that "Being cannot *be* anything but being-with-one-another, circulation in the *with* and as the *with* of this singularly plural existence" (p. 3). "A single being is a contradiction in terms" (p. 12). Here he refers to *we* as a collection of all entities, as in the totality of all beings.

When it comes to discussion of settler/Indigenous relations, however, the notion of ontology gets to the heart of a primary source of our disconnection from one another. In the literature, many have sought to define Indigenous identity by pointing to the ways in which

Indigenous peoples often see themselves as community members first; this is a collectivist standpoint on ontology (Battiste, 2000; Cajete, 2004; Little Bear, 2000; Yazzie, 2000). This community often means more than just the humans with whom we are associated. The *community* also implies the context in which we live, including the land, the water, the air, and the more-than-human occupants of the land. Nothing is separable.

Within Indigenous ontologies, humans are only one factor, no greater or lesser than any other. We may think of this metaphorically as a circle within which exists all of creation in an interconnected web of relationships.

Indigenous ontologies develop to reflect balance in relation to the lands in which they are situated. This is why there is no unifying Indigenous ontology – variations reflect the diversity of Indigenous cultures and knowledges rooted in the lands they have learned to live with. An Inuk's knowledge of seasonal patterns linked to the Arctic is as specific to that region as a Hopi person's understanding of the desert. But the importance of community well-being in each, including people, land, water, and all other creatures, suggests they share this underlying value.

Settler-folk, especially those who have grown up influenced by Western Enlightenment-era thought, favour individualist over collectivist notions. Individual achievement is fundamental to both formal and informal systems of rewards and recognition and is reified within the context of competitions for such. For example, annual institutional awards such as the Academy Awards or the ESPYs, or the Booker Prize single out individuals in recognition of their personal achievements. But no actor ever made it without a screenwriter, director, ward-crew, and so on; no athlete ever made it without the encouragement and support of parents, coaches, trainers, and the like; and certainly, no author ever made it without an editor.

The idea of an award for the achievement of an individual is predicated on the notion that people are separable from social and environmental contexts – a pointed exclusion of the village who raised the child to much acclaim, as it were. It is also a key characteristic of the hierarchic nature of Western ontologies (which can vary in their specificity as much as Indigenous ontologies can). Returning to geometric shapes as metaphors, a triangle in which human beings sit at the apex with all else falling into place beneath illustrates an anthropocentric version of ontology that enables a very different sense of balance centred on individual well-being. This outlook tends to view all else, land, water, and non-human creatures, exclusively in terms of their value as resources to support human activity.

This ontological contrast does not mean we don't share any values – we absolutely do. We all place varying degrees of importance on love, family, friendships, and home. But whether one prioritizes individuality or community more makes a huge difference in how we are in the world. Looking back, we can see clearly how this plays out in the colonial context where the imposition of one way of thinking served to disenfranchise those to whom such thinking was not native, so to speak (Haig-Brown, 2010). The next sections will illustrate more clearly how this is so.

IDENTITY

We are all colonial subjects in Canada, in the sense that we are still very much linked to the Crown of the United Kingdom. And many of us truly treasure that connection. In fact, I, Shannon, know of more than one Indigenous sister who shares my unrepentant love of Coronation Street, Downton Abbey, and Young Victoria, despite what we know our connection to this culture has meant historically for Indigenous peoples. In fact, our identities don't factor at all into the telling of those stories from that small island in the Atlantic. But maybe that's why we like them – at least we are not the ones being picked on and put down, or over-romanticized, in film. We get to sit back and watch for a change, exercising our moral outrage responses at the behaviours of those strange *Others*.

But those stories have something else that Indigenous peoples are only just lately reclaiming loudly for themselves. They are acts of self-representation. British stories about British people, told by Brits. For most of the previous five hundred years since our relationship began, Indigenous peoples have been denied that right through deliberate destruction of evidence shows the complexities of our cultures both at the time of contact and today and through the censure that was affected by our mandatory participation in schools designed to kill both spirit and cultural continuance. Rather, we have the stories of us told through Eurocentric lenses and judged on the basis of Eurocentric values. When stories involving Indigenous characters were told in film, often those characters were not even played by Indigenous people. No small wonder relations between Indigenous peoples and others were strained – Indigenous peoples were not really part of the equation.

Again, we are all colonial subjects. Whether you arrived in Canada at birth or at some point later, your experience of Canada is the direct result of a colonial machine that began its work over four hundred years ago. The machine has been facilitated by ways of thinking and knowing that are exclusively Eurocentric in their construction. After all, the whole colonial project began as an exercise in exploration for resource identification and extraction that would serve the European economy through the wealth development of individual stakeholders. Those notions earlier mentioned, terra nullius and so on, represent a type of ideological domination, which we have noted earlier that Mi'kmaq scholar Marie Battiste (2000) has termed cognitive imperialism. That is, certain truths about Indigenous ways of knowing and being specifically linked to rights to occupation had to be suppressed for colonization to be rationalized in the minds of those who perpetrated and benefited from it.

In the Canadian context, this has led to the entrenchment of an epistemological binary about whose knowledge counts and whose does not. Tim Ingold (2017) suggests that this binary is made explicit within scientific paradigms, which he distils as follows: "On one side of the binary are scientists and other people *of* culture; on the other side are the custodians of traditional knowledge, people *in* culture" (p. 14). Ingold's point is that this binary is false and damaging, but it exists because we are all still subject to it. This is an important point when we consider what the entrenchment of such positioning has meant for Indigenous people over the years. The TRC Report (2015a) is filled with evidence of Indigenous people deliberately being made to feel less-than through a residential school system designed to enact cultural genocide. Very much like the blindness of non-Jewish Germans in the lead up to WWII, non-Indigenous Canadians also had to learn to remain ignorant of the atrocities being committed at those schools because if the schools did their job (which they very nearly did), then the "Indian problem" would be solved and non-Indigenous Canadians stood to continue benefiting. Even within Indigenous families, while the intergenerational impact of surviving residential schools was evident in day-to-day life, the topic was not discussed openly, and many young people didn't know about the true scope and impact of IRSs until they went to university. All of us, Indigenous and non-Indigenous Canadians, had to be brainwashed for the project to be successful, and schools, as Justice Murray Sinclair has noted, were the locus for that process.

One of the key prompts for the title of this chapter, *Think Where You Are*, is the understanding that there is not one square inch of Turtle Island that is not the traditional territory of Indigenous peoples. It is important to know that within the Indigenous populations of Canada, there are a multiplicity of identities and histories, despite certain amounts of commonality. In fact, there are 634 First Nations in Canada, and these Nations speak approximately sixty different languages dispersed throughout twelve major language groups. In British Columbia alone, there are 198 distinct First Nations who speak more than thirty languages. There is a lot of diversity amongst Indigenous peoples.

This means, in part, that the languages of each of these Nations contain cultural ideas and understandings distinct to the peoples who developed and continue to use them and whose lexicons contain regionally specific concepts and knowledges. For example, as described in the previous chapter, the Lil'wat principles of learning (Sanford et al., 2012) offer a clear example of singular words used to describe a state of learning that takes multiple English words to convey. While there are numerous overlaps in values, traditional knowledge, and protocols, there are also significant distinctions in both traditional and contemporary material cultural productions, owing in part to regional variances in the availability of natural resources. That is to say, Indigenous identity is not a monolith, and neither is Indigenous visual expression.

Further, Indigenous politics and political opinion also cannot be construed as monolithic. While there has been significant opposition from Indigenous groups to resource extraction and shipping practices, still other Indigenous Nations embrace the economic advantages that these industries can bring to their communities. In short, it does not serve us to consider Indigenous people as being all the same on any level. What is important to take away from this is the understanding that those colonial roots still tangle up curricula and still promote divisive binaries and cognitive imperialism that continue to affect us/ them notions of Canada, especially where Indigenous Canadians are concerned. Developing decolonial literacy, as we have suggested, is the process of learning to untangle those roots.

PLACE

Land acknowledgements have been received in Canada over the past decade with varying degrees of welcome. They have been welcomed by Indigenous communities as a sign of recognition of our presence, taken up by civic, provincial, and federal governments, universities, and school districts as an act of reconciliation. To many others, however, these acknowledgements are seen as an affront to a status quo they are completely accustomed to and wish to uphold. Still, others have taken up the practice while managing to miss the point entirely, as in the case of the 2019 Toronto Pride Parade in which a land acknowledgement was created but failed to recognize Indigenous presence at all (Friesen, 2019).

The reality is that these land acknowledgements refer to this: *all* land in Canada *is* treatied, unceded, or contested. There are eleven historic treaties in Canada, covering about 50 per cent of the landmass, and twenty-six modern treaties that cover 40 per cent of Canada's landmass. In total, 364 of the 634 First Nation communities in Canada are governed by treaties. Due to some overlap in these numbers, the total area is likely somewhat closer to 70 per cent. The remainder of the country, including most of BC and other areas, Nunavut, parts of Ontario, Quebec, and the Maritimes, are unceded land, meaning that no treaty addressing land use and rights has ever been created with the descendant of original inhabitants.

The notion of *place* is fundamental in how one thinks about the diversity and complexity of Indigenous cultures from region to region around Turtle Island. It is easy to understand how a child who grows up in one place may have the belief that all families are like their family and all communities are like their community. As we grow, however, we learn that families come in many forms, and communities around the world vary significantly. This applies to Indigenous peoples as well. As educators, part of our work in decolonizing our teaching begins with learning about the place(s) on which we live and work and learning about the people who have lived there since before colonial times. *Starting where you are* can also help to debunk pan-Indian notions that have been infused through media, curriculum, and colonial mythologies.

RELATIONSHIP

This brings us to perhaps the most important key idea when it comes to working with Indigenous people, histories, knowledges, and pedagogies: humility. We must, as Dolores van der Wey (2007) phrases it, "know the limits of our knowing" and work towards increasing our understanding by degrees (p. 997). To this end, one of the key strategies we wish to promote with this book is the Friere-ian (1970) notion of problem-based co-learning. That is, we are not calling upon non-Indigenous teachers to become experts in Indigenous subject matters. Rather, we wish to encourage the recognition that there is a lot to know and that it is okay to learn with your students as you work out how to include Indigenous content and pedagogies in your practice.

One of the most effective ways to begin this is to examine one's relationship with being a settler in Canada. Just as many Indigenous communities consider it an important aspect of introductory protocol to situate themselves in relation to their Nation of origin – and to particular families and clans within their Nation, and their situation, especially if they are guests on the territories of another Nation – we encourage settler-folk to do the same. How long has your family been in Canada? Where did they come from? Under what circumstances did they arrive, and what does that mean for you?

> *Leddy: In my work, I give most of my classes an assignment that I hope begins them on a path towards answering these questions. I ask them to think about their favourite place in Canada, being specific about where it is in relation to geography. I ask them to bring up sensory memories of that place as they delve into why that place is special to them. Next, they are asked to do some research into who's traditional territory that place is on, whether or not they are still there, and whether or not there is physical evidence of their historical or contemporary presence. Once they connect these findings with their own family's "arrival" story linked to that*

land, I ask them to create a document, often a video essay, that captures their learning and brings them back to a reconsideration of that place. My goal is not to ruin their fond childhood memories but rather to help them develop a more mature understanding of that place over time. I want to move them into a deeper relationship with place.

One final point to consider here is that humility is also important when searching for resources to bring into your teaching practice. Knowing whose traditional territory you are on will better help you identify resources that honour local histories of occupation, culture, and language and will help to avoid impressions of monolithic ways of being and pan-Indianism. Further, resources that are produced by Indigenous peoples or with significant Indigenous consultation avoid the replication of colonial stereotypes in favour of powerful acts of self-representation. And the type of personal reflection on places as storied beyond our own memories, as in the example above, can help further our journey towards decolonial literacy by tapping into personal connections to the land.

We have offered the thoughts above as a foundation to the work we will do together in this book, recognizing the importance of unpacking the received wisdom of historic curriculum and cultural messaging with which most of us have grown up. This is an important part of the process of engaging in transformative learning, which Mezirow (2009) suggested required the examination of old frames of reference and habits of mind. Such self-examination is also recommended in the context of anti-racist education, exemplified by the work of Ibram X. Kendi and Robin DiAngelo. We need to unpack and re-examine our assumptions about Canada and Indigenous peoples before we can begin to contemplate how to do this work well.

As teachers and writers, we recognize that each of you, Dear Readers, is beginning from a different place. For some of you, the information contained in this chapter is startlingly new, while for others it may present merely a review of the known. Whichever the case, we ask that you keep these things in mind as you work your way through the following chapters. If you find anything rankling as you read, explore your feelings about that and question whether those feelings link to the contents in this chapter. It may be that you have just uncovered another assumption, or it may be that you ate something disagreeable for lunch. It's hard to say from here. But note those moments. They can often show where there is a need to dig in a little deeper.

WEAVING

Before we move on, we wanted to add a few words here about just exactly how we enact the weaving metaphor within our work. As co-authors, we are conscious that our voices are interwoven throughout the text, and even as we each took the lead on various chapters, our editorial process made space for each to make suggestions and additions to one another's chapters. We also sent an early version of the manuscript to a group of Critical Friends, which included four Indigenous educators, one white settler in-service teacher, and another racialized in-service teacher who is a Person of Colour. Using their very thoughtful comments and suggestions and drawing on their wisdom, we revisited our work to strengthen our weave with their words and ideas, felting our ideas more snuggly together. Finally, between each main chapter, we have included mini-chapters that explore the technical stages of weaving to illustrate the interdisciplinary connections that working with Slow and Indigenous pedagogies can offer, especially through project-based and inquiry learning. We hope that readers will take this as inspiration to find ways to bring their own interests into the classroom to create learning experiences that are cross-curricular and make space for Indigenous ways of knowing.

SOURCING AND PREPARING MATERIALS

Before beginning any project, in this case, a weaving (metaphorical or physical), one must settle on the materials needed for the project. In the crafting of this book, we decided to promote a holistic approach to learning rather than provide set lesson plans for replication. In these mini-chapters, we will turn back to our metaphoric weaving, and illustrate a holistic and lived approach to teaching that is project-based, lived, reflects Indigenous ways, and is definitely Slow.

Sourcing materials for weaving, as in our example, involves finding an ethical source of wool fibre. In figures 2.4 and 2.5, local fleece

Figure 2.4. Hand cards and wool by the pond.

Source: Courtesy of Lorrie Miller.

Figure 2.5. Close up of Galiano sheep fleece.
Source: Courtesy of Lorrie Miller.

is shown in an outdoor setting near Duncan, BC. In our region of British Columbia, this is easy to do as there are many local sheep and alpaca farmers that are happy to sell (or even donate) their wool. This connection with local agricultural producers offers students a greater understanding of the processes required to bring material to a current market. Dealing with the local and lived definitely connects to Indigenous ways in that we are attending to the region where we live, the lives of one another in relation to our region, and the other-than-human beings to whom we are all so intimately tied. It also offers an opportunity to consider Indigenous histories, including learning about which Nation's traditional territories all of the associated work is being carried out on, how our modern occupations have impacted the people of that Nation, and what that has meant for land use patterns over time.

Once we have gathered the raw fleece, it needs to be cleaned and processed before it can be spun into yarn. This cleaning is a hands-on process that cannot be rushed. If the yarn is to retain its lanolin for water resistance, then it should be washed with a mild detergent in cold water with very little (or no) agitation. This is patient work, as any agitation can felt the wool, and thus making carding and subsequent spinning very difficult if at all possible.

The manual work of picking and cleaning fleece allows for conversation, stirs curiosity: what do the sheep eat (as you may pick this out of the wool), and where and how do they live, like the grasses, seeds, and burrs evident in the raw fleece? It can also provide an opportunity to experiment with small quantities of the fleece to see how to felt the fleece deliberately by hand with alternating hot and cold water and with a few drops of soap. Students can make felted wool marbles while waiting for the bulk of the fleece to be washed for further preparation. Experienced teachers can probably see here the potential for curricular connections to physics, biology, sustainability, business, physical and health education, and home economics curriculum.

By looking at various examples of sheep locks gathered from different breeds, we can see the length of the fibre staple, the amount of crimp and lustre of the fibres. In contrast, llama and alpaca fleece has no lanolin and is never "greasy" and, as a result, may have insulating characteristics but lacks water resistance. In different areas of Canada, in particular the Pacific Northwest, Indigenous peoples gathered and processed wool for spinning and weaving, depending on what was locally available and at times blended with plant fibres (Olsen, 2010). On the prairies, where sheep and goats were not so common, other textile practices flourished, such as leatherwork, beading, quillwork, embroidery on hide-based cloth, and birch-bark basketry. Attuning to what is naturally local and what is cultivated for our use, all within a sustainable mindset, can be another link to local current, cultural, and historical practices.

Once the fleece is clean and the water runs clear, the fleece can be laid out on racks to drip dry. It is important not to wring it out or to fiddle with it too much at this point as it again risks felting. Once dry, the fleece can be weighed and labelled into manageable bundles of 50,

100, or 125 grams. By the end of this process, students and teachers will be familiar with the feel, weight, and sight of fleece at these different weights and may even be able to estimate the weights by feel and then double-check with a scale. This connects to several aspects of the math curriculum at different grade levels and can apply to biology as well as to process-oriented classes, such as those in technology education, home economics, and visual arts.

To make a single woollen sweater, knit or woven, it will take the fleece of one full-grown sheep, whose fleece has grown for one year. To make a linen shirt, however, one needs about 753 grams of linen thread that has a length of about 10.54 km to weave fabric for the garment. In both cases, resources come from the land, and the fibres are grown and prepared by many individuals with skills in these areas. These are important economic calculations for both producers and manufacturers. Consumers, especially those concerned with reducing their carbon footprint, may also concern themselves with the additional vector of the distance travelled by goods not produced locally.

Further, educators can help students distinguish between natural and manufactured fibres, unpacking the consequences of production for each and connecting that learning to the clothes on their bodies and in the many shops they might frequent. There has been an emphasis on understanding where our food comes from, and attention paid to rising concerns over food sovereignty that have grown with the slow-food movement and the proliferation of school and community gardens. Yet, we still have to make the same kinds of connections with our clothing and other material possessions. Tackling a topic with questions, curiosity, and a framework that responds to the local, ethical, and sustainable, will take you and your students down a path of learning that is bigger than the *how-to* make it, into the question of *why to* make it, and what are the implications for such making.

As a teacher, you have probably learned to plan curricular lessons and units in ways that that respond to two key pedagogical considerations: what are the curricular connections and material outcomes for the lesson or unit you are planning, and how will you assess the student's representation of their learning? Similarly, with a weaving project, one needs to decide the end goal (what is being made), the size of the weaving (how large or small it needs to be), the intent of the cloth (why one is making it). Will it be cut into a garment or hung as decorative work? What is the cultural context for this work? For educators, this means not only the what of curriculum and the *how* of pedagogy but the *why* or theory a well. In business education, it might mean connecting cash handling, marketing, and accounting skills to running the school tuck shop. In sustainability education or biology, it might mean connecting school garden projects to matter cycles, traditional ecological knowledge, and ecosystem complexity, in addition to feeding people.

3

Slow Ways and Indigenous Ways

Miller: It's late June, and I'm sitting in the heart of the Shire (a little communal housing site on Vancouver Island) on a bench hewn from a log with its silvered grain ridged from rains, telling its history of drought and abundance, chill and heat from the change of season over the years. Here is a pond that meanders away from my line of sight, but its inhabitants singing in a morning choir echo off the water and rocks and under the footbridges. The beauty of it all envelops my senses. Red-winged blackbirds, sparrows, starlings, robins, thrushes, kingfishers, a pair of jewelled Anna's hummingbirds, and a solitary Raven overlooks it all. My basket of wool, brushes, and combs for processing fleece into spinnable fibres rest in the long grass next to the bench. Here I comb, brush, spin, knit, all the while listening to the avian chorus and the timbre of bullfrogs. The source of this pond is a spring that feeds the land and all beings and foliage around here, including the house dwellers. It is all rather special with this abundance of life, the slight ripple across the water's surface from an early morning breeze. It is here that I start my day in meditation and appreciation for this all. I am a guest here on this land, and my children are too, as are the "owners" of this special property.

Each day for the past five days has begun precisely like this. Beyond the ferry schedule, I set aside my concern with clock-time. My body tells me when it is time to eat, sleep, sit in silence, wake, walk, and so on. And after five days of being and thinking, I have the volition, and the appropriate time, to put my thoughts into writing. Here I have been sharing my gifts with others who were curious, and I too have learned from them, the magic and medicines abound, such as lavender, mint, juicy radishes from dark soil, wild strawberries, salmonberries, and silence. The wool stories I shared were met with exchanges of alpaca fleece soft as spring bunnies and strong Islandic sheep fleece, skirted yet raw, with pungent lanolin. My hands shone with its oils.

Now that I have set the scene, where is this story going? I note, daily, that all this could have taken place any time over the past hundreds of years, were one to think of it. But it was 2020, amid a massive global pandemic, at a time of unrest as civilians rise-up against the unjust treatment of police against IBPOC. What might this mean for pedagogy and education now and going forward? Also, how can we relate this context to the ideas of slow within pedagogical frameworks?

In this chapter, we will lay out for you the principles of slow thinking and being that inform the threads of the warp that we are weaving into a pedagogical cloth with Indigenous ways of knowing and being. Here we will unpack, layout, expose, tease apart and make sense of the principles of Slow so that it will be clear how they fit ever so perfectly to activate towards decolonizing pedagogies and with the long history of Indigenous thought and pedagogies. To do this, we have turned to Slow movement leaders such as Carl Honoré (2013), who has been instrumental in popularizing the slow movement beyond slow food. Heather Menzies and Janice Newson (2007) uncover the negative impacts of being wired for speed in the university. The work of Berg and Seeber (2017) helps us see what the hope is for improving ways of being in a learning place. We also examined Elaine Lipson's (2012) *Slow Cloth Manifesto* and four key areas she identified as being with one's artistic textile practices (an example of which can be seen in figure 3.1) that lend themselves to a multitude of other practices: process, culture, soul, and materials. We summarized this as follows and make connections beyond the making of cloth in a textile context:

1) The process asks about how we work – this has to do with the ethic and practice of care, skill development, and mastery,
2) Materials require that we consider with what we do work – our need for consideration and awareness of the materials we use to do our work, and the impacts of using such materials,

Figure 3.1. Results of felted and woven collaboration.

Source: Courtesy of Lorrie Miller.

3) Soulful connection to a making practice asks us to reflect on what motivates us to engage in such work and tare about it? What do we wish to express? What about this brings us joy?
4) Community and cultures. Here we consider those with whom we work as this is very relational. We may be learning, teaching, collaborating, exploring on our own, or in a group. We need this connection to place and others and understand the impact this has on our efforts.

Although Lipson discusses time as an aspect of slowness, she notes that it isn't simply about taking more time; it is a recognition that the work we do as humans, the work we undertake, is just that – it is a human endeavour, and as such, it needs to take a human amount of time. We must allow ourselves to sigh and breathe as needed. This offers links to seasonal and cyclical time, or natural time, where things are allowed to take as long as they take, and clock time does not dictate process or completion. Allowing for slowness is also an avenue to genuine mastery, where skills develop at the learner's pace, rather than the pace of a school year calendar.

We want to reiterate that *Indigenous ways of knowing* emerge from distinctly Indigenous world views and not the same Western perspective that ignited the slow movement. We do not aim to place one approach above the other, but rather wish to draw the attention of those familiar with slow ways to the parallels available in Indigenous ways exemplified in the work of Jennifer Adese (2014), Jo-ann Archibald (2008), Gregory Cajete (1994, 2004), Dwayne Donald (2009, 2019), Verna Kirkness (1999), Herman Michell (2018), Robin Wall-Kimmerer (2013), and Matthew Wildcat (2014), to name just a few. We do this with consideration to the concerns raised by Cash Ahenakew (2017) in mind, cautious that "Indigenous knowledges may be instrumentalized or tokenized … depoliticised in ways that fail to disrupt oppressive colonial relations … [or] minimize the complexity of doing this work" (p. 84). Rather, we wish to reveal the complexity through disrupting colonial relations and empowering respectful practices.

We began our search seeking to understand what common underlying principles slow movements have with Indigenous ways. We turned to both scholarly and popular sources for information on these movements, such as slow food, slow travel, slow schools, slow cloth, slow fashion, slow science, along with slow scholarship and Slow pedagogy. Through our readings, we uncovered the following tenets under two overarching themes: a deep ethic of care (including sustainability) and a naturally paced sense of time, separated from standardized clock-time. The tenets of slow under these themes include the following: *experiential* and lived; *place consciousness* where one is connected to the physical place, *deeply relational* where we learn from one another, share knowledge, and attend to social connections, and *connecting inward*, where one attends to one's own emotional, spiritual, soulful self. We will use these tenets as headings in this chapter as we ground these thoughts into existing literature and manifestos from both Western and Indigenous sources. Within each area, the ethic of care and non-clocked time are present. We anticipate that you will also see how the warp of these conceptual threads wind their way into a sturdy weaving with the weft of Indigenous pedagogies when we begin to round the teachings of the Medicine Wheel in our final chapters.

DISCONNECTING FROM THE CLOCK AND CARING DEEPLY

In all of the literature we reviewed, we found that going more deeply into a topic, developing mastery, and coming to understand rather than to simply *knowing* was valued more by those who espouse slowness. Lipson (2012) tells us that "[m]aking things that take attention and care is not a waste of time; it's reclaiming time" (p. 9). This echoes the privileging of time in the learning experience called for by Indigenous ways of knowing and mentioned earlier in this text. Taking the time necessary to learn resonates well with Indigenous approaches to both learning and ceremony, where it is recognized that things take as long as they take. Indigenous science educators Gregory Cajete (1994, 2004) and Robin Wall-Kimmerer (2013) offer rich discussions about the benefits of attending to the pace of things, patient observation, and relational awareness. In her discussion of the traditional process of making black ash baskets, Kimmerer recalls learning from a Knowledge Keeper that a black ash tree will be a basket only when it is ready to be one. In addition to the commonality of taking more or

Figure 3.2. Clock time.

Source: Photo courtesy of Lorrie Miller.

enough time (depicted in figure 3.2), Holt's (2002) philosophy of Slow pedagogy privileges learning deeply, over broadly, and emphasizes the importance of local relevance within a nimble pedagogy. We find the same concepts evident in the work of Goulet and Goulet (2014) as they discuss their model of effective teaching for Indigenous students. For them, "relationship with the student, relationship among students, connection to process, and connection to content" (p. 87) are the key elements that form a healthy learning environment and nurture student learning.

In their publication, *The Slow Professor*, Berg and Seeber (2017) look at the problems associated with time famine in the academy and note that this will never be solved by simply adding more time. They suggest that to effectively challenge "corporate clock thinking" and expectations of productivity, stating "if we think of time only in terms of things accomplished, … we will never have enough of it" (p. 55). In addition to challenging time constructs, Berg and Seeber also uncover ideas of deep care connecting with learning. We can see that slow teaching and Slow pedagogy are not referring to the temporal rate at which a lecture or course is delivered, nor is it about abandoning technology or a return to the *good-ol'-days*. In all of its iterations, slow is also related to the concept of *flow* (Csikszenthihalyi, 1990), in that when one engages in the slow, one can lose one's sense of time – it flies by. It is where the "timeless time" comes into play (Menzies, 2005, Menzies & Newson, 2007; Ylijoki & Mäntylä, 2003).

EXPERIENTIAL

For thousands of years, most teaching and learning across all cultures was done in the context of experience. Humans learned at the knees of their Elders, and knowledge and skills were passed from generation to generation. Scaffolded experiential learning is a mainstay in Indigenous communities, rooted in what one needs to know to live a good life and support the community. Plant knowledge, hunting, weaving, processing meat and hides, carving, beading – each of these aspects of daily life continues to be passed from one generation to the next through teaching linked to doing. This kind of learning is not structured by clock time. In Western contexts, clock time dictates our priorities and erodes the time available for experiential learning. Over time, we have forgotten how we used to learn from one another. We see an opportunity within the notion of Slow to bring experiential learning back to the fore in these contexts.

Slow, whether in food, fibre, travel, schools, or other, is a movement in response to the stresses of our harried lives amid "time poverty" (Berg and Seeber, 2017). Within each slow response is the lived experience of a phenomenon, focusing on the experiential and often the pleasurable. The idea is that if one is exploring a notion, engaging in a task, savouring the making or eating of a meal or whatever, the experience is improved when the stress linked to time constraints is removed. When sufficient time is available for an action to be meaningfully undertaken, more meaning and enjoyment can be derived. Turning to slow schools, Holt (2002) tells us that "doing things slowly is associated with profound pleasure" and suggests that slow school can also be associated with such pleasure (p. 271). In addition, Slow pedagogy offers a needed counter to standards-driven education (Holt, 2002; Payne & Wattchow, 2009), and promotes taking the time to dive deeply into a topic of inquiry. This highlights the need to take sufficient time to learn, to come to know, and understand. For Holt, Slow pedagogy is responsive, flexible, and includes an "imaginative grasp of knowledge and understanding" (Holt, 2002, p. 270). Imagine, for a moment, a school or other place of learning where the students look back on their experiences there as being filled with joy, enriching, and delightful. The notion of profound pleasure should not be foreign nor in opposition to school. Though learning something new may be difficult, and one may experience growing pains that go along with it, we should not shy away from the challenge. We agree with Holt that if we collectively wish for students to "apprehend the variety of human experience and learn how they can contribute to it, we must give them — and their teachers — the opportunity to do so" (p. 271).

This attention to the conditions of learning is central to Indigenous pedagogical approaches. We have referred earlier to the Lil'wat Principles of Learning (Sanford et al., 2012) and draw on them here again to note how they attend specifically to relational considerations such as "acknowledging the felt energy indicating group attunement … seeking places of stillness … [to] stop and listen deeply … [and]recognizing the need to be sometimes in a place of dissonance and uncertainty" (pp. 23–4). Experienced teachers will recognize these as key elements of a good teaching day, but rarely do we take the time to either articulate their occurrence or to overtly plan specifically for their achievement. This points back to the considerations of Goulet and Goulet (2014) around the relational considerations an effective teacher takes into account when working with Indigenous students. As educators, we recognize that expanding our conversations about teaching and learning to deliberately include these relational considerations will benefit all of our students, so we welcome finding parallels here with the tenets of Slow as well.

Seeber and Berg collate examples of pedagogical approaches that bring courses alive for university students that include not just storytelling in a course but storytelling *a course*. Berg and Seeber (2017) turn to the work of Searle-White and Crozier as they discuss how storytelling in a course differs greatly from lecturing in that it is a responsive, nuanced, embodied narrative where the teller responds and adjusts to the listener. In such a situation, the teacher can bring their passion for the subject and breathe life into it for the students, and the students experience the story and the learnings derived from the narratives. Of course, storytelling is a key element of Indigenous pedagogies as well. Thomas King (2003) wrote extensively about the importance of stories in his celebrated Massey Lecture, *The Truth About Stories*, suggesting that in the end, that is all we are. Jo-ann Archibald has also written extensively in *Indigenous Storywork* (2008) about the importance and function of traditional stories drawing from the stories of Elders in her Sto:lo community. Her research reflects one of the most important reasons for telling stories in Indigenous learning, making meaning, which she describes as "a process that involves going away to think about their meanings in relation to one's life" (p. 90). In other words, the introspective aspect of learning from stories can be a slow process.

For Phillip G. Payne and Brian Wattchow (2009), Slow pedagogy is one where the body is integral to the learning experience. For them, "a slow pedagogy, or eco-pedagogy, allows us to pause or dwell in spaces for more than a fleeting moment, and therefore, encourages us to attach and receive meaning from that place" (p. 16). As outdoor environmental educators and researchers, they tell us that outdoor, physical, health, and sustainability education is too frequently stuck in a cultural logic limited to skilled activities and safe performance in the outdoors. They also critique the over-reliance on technology undermines intents behind environmental education; they feel that the "'fast' trajectory in environmental education constitutes another means through which the prospects of experiential education are being diminished, via the disembodiment, displacement, disembedding and decontextualizing of varied face-to-face interactions and relations with others, including 'nature'" (p. 17). In particular, Payne and Wattchow see a Slow eco-pedagogy of place applied to experiential education as an alternative to fast pedagogies in education.

Similar concerns are found in Indigenous approaches such a land-based pedagogies. Herman Michell (2018) points to the Western philosophical traditions that underpin many approaches to environmental and eco-education. Positivist and individualist perspectives rooted in Enlightenment thinking tend to view land as a commodity or a source of recreation. His assertions are mirrored in the earlier work of Lucie Sauvé (2005), who mapped out fifteen approaches to environmental education and drew much the same conclusion regarding those rooted in this way. In land-based learning approaches, Indigenous perspectives that attend to cycles in nature over time and the inter-relationship of all elements of and beings on the land have patience and observation at their heart, rooted more in holistic and relational thinking.

Experiential, hands-on, kinesthetic learning are all ways to understand getting our hands messy with the business of education. Though one's imagination plays an important role in learning, there are times where we need to try things out for ourselves, to feel new knowledge in a lived way. Let's take a look at a science experiment exploring the basics of gravity, for example, where one can learn about all objects falling at the same rate. How meaningful is this for the learner when the "facts" are simply read, heard, or even observed compared to trying it out for oneself? The experience of listening or watching the brick and penny drop, feeling the weight of each object in one's hands, listening as they hit the ground – this experience is tangible, possibly even fun. In another example, we can look at food production and cooking. Slow food advocates certainly have awakened many to the joys found in careful and considered meal production. The value is not in how quickly or efficiently one makes a meal; it is more in the care of growing, harvesting, foraging, and then creating and sharing that is of greater value. As Goulet and Goulet (2014) point out, "respect for resources is taught when students have manipulatives and concrete materials. Social skills are reinforced since students are expected to share materials" (p. 92). This applies in the Grades 9–12 cooking classroom, as equally as it does in the classrooms of primary grades and all classrooms in between.

With our academic and creative roots in the visual arts, the hands-on approach is a vital part of learning. Textile arts educator Mary-Lou Trinkwon (2010) calls into question the romanticized do-it-yourself movement where the focus is on *doing* without discipline.

She questions the motives of post-secondary institutions to close programs that include disciplines such as textiles even when there is student demand for this learning, leaving a pedagogical void for those seeking to learn without institutions. As an instructor, she was challenged by students who said they'd *seen the how-to already on You-Tube*, which points out the relational importance between teacher and learner that extends beyond a one-sided presentation of instruction. Trinkwon says that though she is not a textile arts master, she sees the relationship between the student and instructor as vital and the classroom as a transitional space. She tells us: "I enter the classroom as myself and I can't help be influenced and impacted by all the others, the knowledges and conditions that I find there and take up there" (p. 5). This passage says a lot about the need for Slow pedagogy, with a connection to one another, self, materials, place, practices, and time and resonates strongly with the four pedagogical concerns for effective teaching raised by Goulet and Goulet (2014).

Brian Wattchow (2001) challenges common outdoor education assumptions and practices regarding interpreting the experience, the environment and the body. He concludes that our collective well-being, both our world and us, are not separable from our "technological life-world." As such, technological mediated experiences need to consider one's lived experience when engaging, in or designing for outdoor education. Wattchow also warns that it will not be possible to fully relearn skills, crafts, and related embodied knowledge that are currently being lost. He reminds us of something familiar, even if distant:

> When someone is seen practicing their craft, it refers to a way of Being centred in becoming through making with care. This transaction almost always requires the use of tools and techniques, which always shape the user's Being – functionally, morally, and symbolically. When a craft is performed with care and virtuosity it is a form of applied ecology (Fry, 1992). It coalesces in a healthy body, technologically engaged in-and-with a healthy community and environment. (Wattchow, 2001, p. 23)

We agree with Wattchow's observations and call for the continued support of learning art and craft with one's own hands and body, hoping that through one's skilful, *careful* interaction with the world, we can foster a healthy, healthful place in the world. Experiential learning opportunities are also a key aspect of Indigenous pedagogies. Learning that is connected to what students need to know to become self-sufficient and good community members is a fundamental goal of Indigenous education (Little Bear, 2000). Michell's (2018) work lists multiple ways in which land-based approaches infuse experiential learning across curricular areas as a holistic approach to both curriculum and pedagogy.

LAND CONSCIOUS/PLACE CONSCIOUS

Place-based education is a term that many may already know; learning responds to the physical place where the learners are situated, including culture, geography, geopolitical region, and seasonality (Payne & Wattchow, 2009). Deep care and an emotional, sometimes spiritual, connection to a place *is* place consciousness. Kimberley Holmes and Carl Leggo (2019) tell us that "[o]ur human lives are interconnected spiralling stories strands encompassing complex existence" (p. 281). Theirs is a poetic place and time in the world. For us, place consciousness means that we consider the land upon which we now reside, the lands from where we came, the places we call home, knowing that these are complex intersections that hold life and story for many more than just us. As artists, this connection to the land means respecting and treating holistically the materials we use in our artmaking and mindfully disposing of any unused or residual materials in a project. We know that there is no such place as *away*, so we can never truly throw something *away*. Away, it seems, is home to someone, something else, and so we act accordingly in our making and teaching others. We only need to look at the impacts of fast fashion and the irreparable damage to river ecosystems and adjacent communities in the dumping of chemical dyes, as poignantly illustrated in the 2017 documentary film by David McIlvride and Roger Williams, *RIVERBLUE*.

In thinking about how to be conscious of land in our pedagogies, we attend to the principles of respect and reciprocity in how we choose to select and dispose of the materials we work with, and appreciate Wall-Kimmerer's (2013) framing of this as an ethic of conservancy from an Indigenous perspective. In considering what the rules for an "honourable harvest" might be, she notes, "never take the first or the last. Take only what you need. Take only that which is given. Never take more than half. Leave some for others ... never waste what you have taken" (p. 183). Learning to view oneself as part of nature rather than in charge of it can make a huge difference in how we perceive and interact with the land on which we live and evokes our responsibility to maintain good relations with it.

Place consciousness in Slow pedagogy means knowing what appropriate subject matter is for this location, at this time, for these learners. We turn to the notion of the fibreshed, a related but different field from pedagogy. Like slow food, the fibreshed movement is inspired by the same roots. Where one concerns itself with the farming practices of food crops and accessibility, the other focuses on the production and making of textiles in a local area. Burgess (2019) identifies a fibreshed as place-based textile sovereignty that considers and includes the regional plants, animals, cultural and artisan practices. Within a fibreshed, there needs to be a transparency of the origin of the materials and processes in its production into textiles. In particular, there is an emphasis on "the *connectivity* among all parts, from soil, to skin and back to soil" (p. 7). We see this as being highly related to Slow pedagogy and other slow movements, in understanding the material source, which is similar to place consciousness, and material relationality, along with connectivity, where generations of communities in an area have created textiles with fibres from their local livestock, and cultivated crops, regardless of the fibre source (alpaca, sheep, goat, or cotton, hemp, flax), processed with traditional or modern means and coloured with locally derived plant dyes.

Gregory Cajete (2004) often writes about the importance of recognizing the interconnection of all things to highlight our role as humans in participating in the maintenance of balance. Metaphysically, or perhaps metaphorically, he frames our world as the product of "chaos, and its offspring, creativity ... the generative forces of the universe" (p. 48). Each of us is subject to and ourselves generative of these forces, so our ways of being in the world must reflect our responsibility to keep them in balance through our actions. Leroy Little Bear (2000) offers that "the function of Aboriginal values and customs is to maintain the relationships that hold creation together. If creation manifests itself in terms of cyclical patterns and repetitions, then the maintenance and renewal of those patterns is all important" (p. 81). In considering the state of our global climate, connecting the last century or so in terms of how we have attended to our world with our responsibility for maintaining it makes some of our key failures in this relationship clear. Holistic perspectives such as those above can help us recalibrate and reposition ourselves to do better collectively moving forward. This is a key parallel between Slow and Indigenous ways. Time and attention are required if we are to, as Archibald (2008) suggests, act in ways that honour "the synergistic influence of and our responsibility toward the generations yet to come. The animal/human kingdoms, the elements of nature/land, and the Spirit World are an integral part of the concentric circles" (p. 11) of holistic and relational thinking.

In addition to the growing and making of textiles from local sources, a fibreshed, like Lipson's (2012) slow cloth manifesto, expresses a mandate to learn with openness from others and share one's teachings with others. There is a responsibility to reciprocity – to give back and only take what is needed within this framework. Burgess (2019) tells about her fibreshed via her narrative of a journey into fibresheds globally. When we analyze her words here, we see a great overlap with this movement and some of the underlying values in Slow and Indigenous pedagogies. Burgess shares with her readers one of her greatest lessons on her journey was in realizing that we can bring about solutions to some of the globe's greatest current challenges about climate change and wealth inequities when empowered communities can forge livelihoods in ways that connect them to their land, and to sustainable material practices, in ways that honour and sustain their cultural heritage. This illustrates the importance of human communities' connection to their land, culture, and tradition. In addition, she advocates for:

> Ongoing learning from regional indigenous communities, whose understanding of the human role in the ecosystem is unparalleled. From these local inquiries we've established what is an ever-growing understanding of the practices required to rebuild our soil, heal our climate and strengthen our regional economies. The methods we've begun to utilize to generate globally impactful place-based solutions include developing bodies of site-specific research that help us measure the comate impact of soil-to-skin processes and develop appropriately scaled open-sourced technologies. (p. 13)

Although Burgess does not address schooling specifically, the call for sharing craft and textile process skills and learning from local artisans, whether weavers, dyers, sheep, or flax farmers, will certainly resonate with teachers. Here we see that fibreshed work is indeed related to pedagogy. Here we have examples of experiential, hands-on learning that pays attention to the location, both in geography and in time, and is deeply relational to the land, materials used, and the people involved. As we suggested in the previous chapter, this call to learn from regional Indigenous communities is an important one for educators. *Thinking where you are* means building connections with and relationships with local Indigenous knowledges, pedagogies, and people in ways that are inclusive, respectful, reciprocal, and of great mutual benefit to all of our students.

This way of thinking, this ecology of concepts and content, applies across curricular areas. At its core, this is about connecting content, what goes into informing it, and where it can be applied. As we have suggested elsewhere, this is a key aspect of Indigenous knowledges and pedagogies too. For learning to have real value, it must connect to our students' lives and lived experiences, rooted in real-world skills and considerations. In other words, the students themselves form a part of the curricular content of their learning. Financial literacy, for example, is part of the Grade 7 math curriculum in BC because we live in a world where money is a reality, so our students need to understand how to manage money in their lives. Likewise, with career education at the secondary level, a range of learning goals can be connected, including personal goal setting, understanding local opportunities and global needs, and valuing volunteer engagement. Collaboration is an integral part of high school career education, which drives home the importance of making and maintaining positive relationships. Networking is not simply a self-serving endeavour but a reciprocal way of being, a connected way of being.

We recently received an email from a past student whom we worked and collaborated with during an education conference. She shared with us a short introductory video she'd created for her students, and she wanted to let us know the connection she carried with her from our work together into her teaching practice. In the video, she illustrates how students and teachers together can honour the land they are on, thinking about the multiple connections to the land

and cultures of those who have long resided there and the learning activities that can come out of it. Her example was of weaving yarn with found sticks or twigs. The end product may be a woven and painted stick. But the learning goes beyond the end product into the time spent outdoors, the conversations about place and history, the grounding of one's learning in lived experience.

DEEPLY RELATIONAL

Whether they are human or greater than human beings, all our relations reside alongside us and are at the forefront of relationality within Indigenous and Slow pedagogy. Not only do we care about those with whom we work, those whom we teach, those from whom we learn, but we also feel a relation to the materials with which we work. Recall when you were working with a material, perhaps clay, cloth, or a basket of fresh strawberries. The more familiar the materials, the greater connection one has with the material and process. Over some time, working with others and with materials develops a greater understanding of the qualities of each. When teaching others, we remind ourselves and our students that we teach people, not subjects. One may lecture about subjects, but the act of teaching is a relational one in which engagement with others about a topic moves the learning forward rather than the topic itself. In other words, our students need us to teach them in relatable ways. So, relating to students and supporting their learning is critical for understanding our work as educators and scholars. There is a responsibility that goes along with pedagogy – and that is to be committed to sharing your knowledge and skills and imparting responsibility for others to do the same. Our goal is to engage others with their learning and skill development journey so that they can share their learning, whether as a teacher, mentor, or peer. We are always learning; whether or not we are mindful of such learning is another matter altogether.

Outdoor and environmental place-based pedagogy has called for Slow with principles that Maurice Holt (2002) refers to a *less is more* approach to learning, opting for depth of learning over a period of time, and allowing for understanding to develop rather than filling up quickly on the volume of information. We need to bring students to care about what they are learning. Care about the topic links to our earlier notes from Berg and Seeber (2017), as well as Michell (2018) and Wall-Kimmerer (2013). We, like Holt, Cajete (1994), Payne (2005), and Payne and Wattchow (2009), call for land-based and experiential learning that can bring understanding through art, song, movement, poetry, or story, showing how a multitude of expressive means can represent knowledge and understanding. As do Sanford et al. (2012), they call for connecting to others than one's self. Payne and Wattchow call for attention to the Indigenous peoples in their area near Melbourne to appreciate and wonder about the historical and cultural dimensions of place and contested territory through the deliberate inclusion of locally rooted Indigenous histories. Their Slow pedagogy "works to displace numerous dualisms and disconnections that still abound in environmental education: the body and mind; I, we and the world; self and other; ontology and epistemology; and as a result, potentially offers some partial reconciliation of inner, social, and outer natures; theory and practice; indoor/class and outdoor/field; epistemology and ontology" (Payne & Wattchow, 2009, p. 30). Their work here echoes the voices of many Indigenous Elders on this continent who remind us again and again that we are all related, and our responsibility is to maintain good relations through seeking balance (Archibald, 2008; Michell, 2018; Wall-Kimmerer, 2013). In revealing the preoccupation with economic growth that often fuels Western curricular concerns, Dwayne Donald (2019) envisions instead "an educational project committed to acknowledging and honouring the complex connectivities that human beings have to the abundant more-than-human entities that live among us" (p. 104). We really have a lot on our plates.

INTERNAL CONNECTION

Connecting to your own emotional and spiritual self is also a part of both Indigenous and Slow pedagogy. Our inner world is profoundly personal and significant. But, too often, we ignore it in formal education since the seriousness of learning has long been considered exclusively as the realm of the mind with little connection to heart, body, or spirit. For example, public schools in Canada are strictly non-denominational in most provinces; if one chooses to go to a faith-based school, a private school may be the only option. However, one's spirit and emotion are not really considered essential aspects of connecting with mind, curiosity, and learning. For instance, as a learner or a teacher, you will likely be able to recall a time when you either experienced enthusiasm or witnessed the excitement of someone else, when a topic evoked genuine care and passion, or when engaging in a learning activity with others who care about one another. Such moments evoke both pleasure and a sense of flow and deep engagement. When a teacher cares about the topic they teach, students notice this passion. If the teacher has also established a caring classroom environment, the students may also catch this enthusiasm.

How do we hold a space so that our students may explore curiosity or creativity, where a teacher may model reflection, vulnerability, and authority? St'at'imc Elder Gerry Oleman, who often visits our Indigenous education classes at UBC, teaches us that we each have a special gift. Part of our job as humans is to figure out what that is to be our best selves and serve our community. As teachers, making space and time for our students to explore and reflect is one way we can help them find their special purpose. It moves our work beyond curricula and into living. We need to look for opportunities that bring enjoyment to learning and feed curiosity linked to our students' interests. We need to think about how we can situate our teaching and learning outside the boundaries of school walls where our lives are actually lived, as Goulet and Goulet (2014) and Michell (2018), and a host of other Indigenous scholars suggest.

We are certainly not the first educators to suggest this link between teaching and learning and pleasure. We recall again Berg and Seeber (2017), who tell us that "when one enjoys teaching, one does it well" (p. 34). They go on to suggest that it is possible that enjoyment in a learning situation by both teacher and student is a predictor of positive learning outcomes. We find this curious. What is it about our own pleasure in teaching and engagement with the subject that transmits to our students? We think perhaps the answer can be found in Indigenous pedagogy. Little Bear (2000) suggests, for example, that sharing is part of developing good feelings in Indigenous communities, referring to both the materials and intangibles of daily life. Wall-Kimmerer (2013) also suggests that learning to understand the harmonious interrelations of the world around us reinforces our connection to one another and evokes the positive responsibility to maintain good relations.

Berg and Seeber (2017) "believe that we can combat stress and cynicism while keeping ourselves alive by promoting pedagogy of pleasure" (p. 35). In addition to this, they refer to brain research that has shown the inherent connection of one's emotion to one's thinking and decision-making. Intelligence, they tell us, is situational. Thinking and learning can only happen from within our bodies, and our bodies experience the world around us in a particular place, time, and circumstance. They draw upon the work of Antonio Damasio, who found that when one's frontal cortex is damaged (one's emotion centre in the brain), then not only were emotions adversely affected, in a severe case, absent, the ability to make a decision was also affected. This means that not only do our emotions colour our decisions and thinking, they are also *required* to think and to make new decisions. This is borne out of Shannon's research into humour in education (Leddy, 2018; Leddy & O'Neill, 2022), and we know from our reading of Little Bear (2000), Drew Hayden Taylor (2006), and Vine Deloria Jr. (1969) that humour is indeed fundamental in maintaining good relations.

One of the reasons we wanted to include the holistic framework of the Medicine Wheel in our work responds directly to the importance of connection. If we consciously factor in all aspects of our students as humans by including spiritual and emotional considerations in our planning and teaching, we can engender rich and connected learning environments where students are willing to be creative and to take risks in their learning. Carl Honoré (2013) tells us that "[w]hen we are calm, unhurried and free from stress and distractions, the brain slips into a richer more nuanced mode of thought" (p. 66). This slow thinking offers more time on a problem and an opportunity for creative designing, problem-solving, and knowledge creation. Honoré calls for an abolishment of the "taboo" over slowness. He says that "[w]e need to accept that decelerating judiciously, at the right moments, can make us smarter" (p. 67). This reminds us of the importance of wait time in teaching, and we know that for many students, including many Indigenous students, this can be a crucial aspect of pedagogy in allowing students the time it takes to form and explain their thoughts. In Indigenous communities, as Archibald (2008) notes, "silence is respectful and can create good thinking" (p. 89). Many students will have learned from their Elders the discipline of learning "not to speak until they were sure about their answers" (p. 89). Imagine the difference that recognizing this in our students could make in how we approach teaching them.

Berg and Seeber (2017) look at the emotional language students used to describe positive learning experiences: "inspiring," "stimulating," "engaging," "thought-provoking." The students did not separate how they felt and what they thought about a course or topic. Seeber and Berg found that regardless of whether students liked or disliked a course or topic, their emotions were integral to their learning. We wonder, can schools become brave spaces, places of vulnerability, where risk-taking in learning leads to creative or rich learning outcomes? Further, we wonder if moving towards pedagogies that honour process over outcomes (Goulet & Goulet, 2014; Regnier, 1994) might also promote deeper learning connections and those feelings of engagement we know are so important.

In teacher education, we have been asking and guiding teacher candidates to be reflective on their practices to create safe and positive learning environments for their child and youth learners in schools. Indeed, the curriculum in our province of British Columbia has opened a space for curiosity, time for reflection and exploration of ideas, and rich learning. Our teacher candidates are also asked (throughout their eleven-month condensed teacher education program) to engage in an inquiry of their teaching practices in the hopes that they will develop an inquiry disposition as they enter their careers. Yet, such a task of deep consideration takes time and focused attention. In any time-condensed learning environment, we wonder if one can truly both hurry-up and reflect deeply?

We are connected to the relational and the lived learning experience. It is where Ayers et al. (2017) show how meaningful use of art engagement in a classroom setting can slow a typical rushed school day to make learning more meaningful. When making art, one takes time to build, consider, share, discuss, reflect, revise, remake and so on, until the work is finished satisfactorily to the feelings and thoughts of the maker, in conversation with leaders, teachers, mentors. We need to allow the time that it takes to learn, to be with the ideas, to create. This response to our rushed, hurried world is a reminder that "learning takes patience and time" (Chrona, 2014). Slow teaching, Ayers et al. tell us, can also be a form of teaching for social justice. We must take that to heart when teaching others and when learning ourselves. Growth takes time. If what we seek is growth, understanding, and transformation, then we must also allow for and provide the time needed for such an undertaking.

Slow and Indigenous pedagogies encourage the deep dive into a topic to stay with the question long enough to develop an understanding and integration of this knowledge. For Menzies and Newson (2007), this holds implications for the university instructor and researcher; where there is a return to sustained dialogue with an emphasis on knowledge *creation* rather than knowledge *production* that is "more narrowly focussed on gathering data, processing information and packaging it as knowledge" (p. 69). This resonates with the practice of Indigenous *storywork* (Archibald, 2008), in which the cyclical repetition of stories leads community members to meanings that build in layers over time. Deep dialogue, knowledge creation, and connection building all require a certain amount of time that is often in contrast to the lived experience of scholars and instructors, where external time pressures hinder these pursuits. In Indigenous societies, that has long been the way that knowledge is built and transmitted, and it remains so today for certain skills and teachings (Adese, 2014; Cajete, 1994; Michell, 2018).

Time pressures and conflicting time perspectives that impede learning and relationship building are well discussed by scholars Ylijoki and Mäntylä. (2003) who identify such time conflicts amongst lived experiences of academics. They identify types of time in their research: 1) scheduled time, 2) contracted time, 3) personal time, and 4) timeless time. The idea of timeless time, where one is so engrossed in the pursuit of enjoyment (whether that be creative, intellectual, or physical), is clearly linked to the idea of flow (Csikszentmihalyi,1990). Ylijoki and Mäntylä's interviewees generally struggled with balancing work time and personal time, whether work time was made up of contracted time or scheduled time, where contracted time is bound by the terms of a finite contract and contains all the pressures associated with temporary work, while scheduled time is bound by teaching and meeting obligations. The temporal order of their work environments at universities, as governed by university management, emphasizes productivity and efficiency and where time is quite literally seen as money, so that: "[t]he academics' everyday work has to be transformed into quantifiable measures and results irrespective of the internal rhythms of the work itself" (p. 74). Central to this is their question resulting from their research: what can we do to reconcile these constructed time conflicts to allow for "more space for timeless time, flexibility in schedules, security in employment and balance in our personal time" (p. 75)?

Recall the discussion at the beginning of this book about seasonal and cyclical time. We connected this to the way in which we move around the Medicine Wheel, clockwise, following the sun in resonance with teachings from the Nations of the Plains where the wheel comes from. When we are attuned to the world, we don't need a clock to tell us when we should eat or a calendar to tell us when to harvest our tomatoes. The Indigenous understanding of time, of natural time, is to live in a state of flow. It is not clock bound; it is about living in our bodies in the world. As Cajete (2004) suggests, "the flux, or ebb and flow, of chaos appears in everything and envelops us at all time and in all places" (p. 48).

The deep dive that Menzies and Newson call for links closely to Nakamura and Csikszentmihalyi's (2014) concept of *flow*. Likewise, flow is clearly related to Ylijoki and Mäntylä's notion of *timeless time*. To best unpack the idea of flow, we turn to Nakamura and Csikszentmihalyi, who consider flow as an intentional process including intense concentration. And although the concept of flow is multifaceted, the connections between slow and flow occur in the individual experience of a phenomenon. Nakamura and Csikszentmihalyi (2014) tell us that "[w]hen attention is completely absorbed in the challenge at hand, the individual achieves an ordered state of consciousness. Thoughts, feelings, wishes, and actions are in concerns. Subjective experience is both differentiated and integrated, the defining qualities of a complex phenomenon" (p. 244). The authors go on to identify two types of interventions that link to flow principles. One intervention is where one plans activities or environments to foster or encourage engagement at a flow level, and the other is where one assists another to achieve flow. The key in all flow engagement is the level of intrinsic motivation where one is engaged in activities of their personal interest and unencumbered by external demands or time.

Flow is certainly not a state of being or engagement that is limited to the solo actor. In fact, we recall again the work of Sanford et al. (2012) and the emphasis their work places on attending to group energy and attunement – that, we feel, is the very definition of flow. Flow is often the glue in a group, where all are working towards a goal, such as in an animated and knowledgeable conversation or an inspired music jam session. This is where a group clicks and results in a greater understanding or a richer creation.

This brings us to the question: So, what? We've long known that when one has a goal that is burning, getting into a space for a duration may result in amazing work if conditions are right. We also know of "blocks" that may hinder a writer, musician, or artist, even without outside distraction. Inspiration, it would seem, is also required to produce flow, not simply time, materials, and a lack of distraction.

Slow pedagogy and Indigenous pedagogies do more than open opportunities for experiencing flow. They can, in fact, challenge the colonizing impacts of linear time by encouraging physical and spiritual ways of knowing and being that disrupt the mind/body dualism. Shahjahan (2015) suggests that by slowing down, we can "re-embody the body in the learning environment." (p. 495), suggesting that we can privilege the quality of attention on a topic, skill, subject, or question, rather than evaluating it by "time-on-task." By decolonizing time, opening up our own understanding of time beyond clock-time, we allow ourselves to reconnect with our physical being, acknowledge our lived experiences, and engage in the depths of our work. Slow and Indigenous pedagogies provide time to think, to digest, to dialogue. With such a pedagogy, we allow for serendipity, like with an old-fashioned library *shelf-search* when seeking a needed book yields to thumbing through others on the shelf by authors not previously known. Though online library searches may find other books with the same or similar keywords, there is no guarantee.

Slow, as we have come to understand various slow movements, are not merely the opposite to fast. Slow involves a way of being in the world, one that is thoughtful, engaged, located, relational, and reflective; it is praxis. One cannot simply theorize about slow. In order to really understand slow, one must do and be in a *slow* way. Similarly,

Indigenous ways of learning and knowing are not simply opposi-
tional to traditional Western education practices. Rather, they have
developed over time and in place contexts. We see them as a complement to Western thinking that affords even deeper understanding and
connection.

> *Miller: An irony that I cannot escape even as I draft these pages is my
> lack of sleep, my fitful nights and my ruminating brain. I resisted the
> urge to write this all down with the quickest of my capacity, for I know
> that this is not the way to be with ideas. So, to force and slow my process
> of engaging in contemplation, I have taken to using paper notebooks and
> pen. This handwriting, unto its self, allows a feeling of achievement as
> I move through the pages; by doing this, I must consider words as I put
> them on paper. I must render the words and, therefore, the thoughts with
> both physical and cognitive clarity. In this way, when it comes time to
> transcribe these pages to a digital document, I hope to be able to read and
> understand this scrawl.*
>
> *By closing my backlit screen and opting for paper, it is more of a
> physical experience that differs from my daily desk work. It is slower
> as words per second per minute added to a page, but this is, after all,
> not a race. This is most certainly a journey. Thankfully, it is not in any
> way, a solo journey, one that I share with my writing partner and my
> sister-scholar.*

In the following chapters, we connect each quadrant of the Medicine Wheel to the realities of teaching, highlighting some of the aspects
of humanity we have previously ignored in our professional practice.
We move clockwise through the wheel, following the path of the sun.
We begin in the East, where each new day is born.

But first …

SPINNING

Spinning fibre into yarn inherently utilizes a wheel, whether a whorl
on a spindle (figures 3.3 and 3.4) or a wheel moved by hand, foot or
machine. The act of spinning wool, in our ongoing example, imbeds a
twist into a loose fleece that has been prepared by carding or combing

Figure 3.3. Bobbin with wool on spinning wheel.

Source: Photo courtesy of Lorrie Miller.

to align the fibres until they are somewhat parallel. The twist in the fibres will determine the strength and the loftiness or warmth. The amount of air allowed into the twisted fibre dictates whether it is a woollen or a worsted yarn. Woollen is warmer and softer but less durable than the worsted, which is not as warm but is sturdier and better for outer clothing.

It is fun to experiment with wool roving and strength testing, and this offers plenty of connections to math and science curriculums. Roving is a long, combed bit of wool fleece – its natural state before being felted or spun. It can be easily broken by hand when pulled apart.

Figure 3.4. Wound ball of yarn and spindle.

Source: Photo courtesy of Lorrie Miller.

But, when twisted until it is smooth to touch, it becomes very hard to pull apart. Students can easily feel this strength. A force test could be measurable in a science class (at any level) and further extended by looking at the strength of various other natural and manufactured fibres. In addition, looking at these fibres under a magnifying glass or microscope will reveal key differences in their properties and affordances. Physics, technology education, and outdoor education enter the picture when we consider the transformation of roving to woollen thread – this presents opportunities for learning about how ropes are constructed and how to improve their tensile strength.

While the science implications relate to the material's testable and measurable features, we can also turn to history and literature for spinning stories. Think of mythological spinners, such as the Greek tale of Arachne or the famed rascal of Grimm lore, Rumpelstiltskin. Another area of connection that may be less obvious within this is the relation-ship between physical education and spinning. The act of spinning on a wheel requires coordination of movement, attention to rhythm, and persistence to see a spool fill, which also creates connections to music and dance education. Spinning with a spindle requires coordination, attention, and persistence, but it is more like working a yoyo with a productive outcome – not just entertainment. The coastal peoples in British Columbia are well known for their giant spindle whorls and resultant large-diameter yarn and woven cloaks. Contemporary Musqueam spinner and weaver, Debra Sparrow's work is exhibited at UBC and elsewhere. Visual artist Susan Point, also of Musqueam, has her spindle whorls on display at the Vancouver International Airport in Richmond.

There are connections here beyond the simple mechanics of spin-ning as well – let's look at Robotics 11, with Applied Design from the British Columbia curriculum. This curriculum requires prototyping, analysis of design, user-centred research, and empathetic observation (and more). To understand the big ideas and curricular goals via a slow and Indigenous approach, we look at elements identified within the existing curriculum: empathy, care of and for the user, collabora-tion on a project, prototyping, and understanding of the controlling systems and torque, friction, traction, and design for the life cycle. This is just a little bit of what the curriculum entails, but these big ideas can be definitely understood within the framework we propose here. Such course content has inherently a holistic approach with mul-tiple factors incorporated into the learning design. Teams are formed, projects planned, experiments tested and retested, observations made, and projects refined. To take this further, one needs to ask why is this project undertaken in the first place? What are the possible positive and negative impacts of said projects? What is gained from learning beyond mechanical production? Here we look at the healthy function-ing of teams, the relationships formed, with mentors and mentees col-laborating. Then we can look further to implications for climate action, sustainability, alternate energy sources, recycling and reuse of materi-als previously cast aside. Again, learning collaboratively in an authen-tic learning community is an important part of this approach and can be the foundation for learning in this and many other curricular areas.

4

East – Spiritual – Respect

East, this is where the sun rises, and the day begins. East on the Medicine Wheel is associated with yellow and signifies the *spiritual* (figure 4.1). The symbolism of the East is rich and plentiful, including the direction of birth, renewal, trust, and hope. It is the direction of light, courage, clear vision, and service. It is a beginning. As we look at the Medicine Wheel given to all of us in *The Sacred Tree* (Lane et al., 1984), there are foundational considerations we need to take to heart. As you read, keep in mind that the wholeness of the Medicine Wheel remains even when it is divided into quadrants – the boundaries are as distinct as those between winter and spring. Given that this book and these teachings are for people, the focus here is on human development in the fullest sense.

Words have power, and so we do not use the word spirit lightly. So, for you fellow spirits who are challenged or made uncomfortable by this very notion, we would like to put the following ideas forward as they are teachings that have helped shape and guide our text. If you find yourself uncomfortable with the idea of a spirit or a soul, consider it as your *anima* or *pneuma*, which keeps your body from being a corpse – your very own life-force. This notion of life-force is global, albeit with varying understandings, traditions, and practices. For those who do not have a faith tradition, the notion of one's inner *spirit* may hold an abstract and possibly dogmatic connotation. Benjamin Bloom (1956) created a holistic taxonomy of learning that

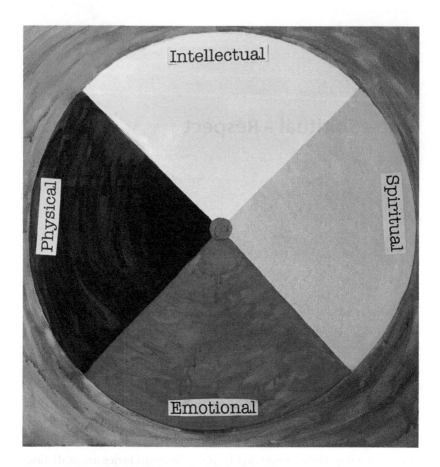

Figure 4.1. Medicine Wheel facing East, Spiritual, Yellow.

Source: Courtesy of Shannon Leddy.

avoided spirit altogether by offering only three domains: the cognitive, affective and psychomotor. Bloom's Taxonomy has been very influential in the area of teaching and learning for over 40 years. Each of these maps well onto the Medicine Wheel, as Lefever (2016) points out, matching the cognitive domain to the intellectual, the affective to the emotional quadrant, and the psychomotor to the physical. But as an insight offered by one of her students revealed, it is the spiritual that is missing here, leaving Bloom's model just short of a complete vision.

In the East, we address spirit outside of dogma but rather in connection with the capacities described in *The Sacred Tree*. We can react to that which is non-material through abstractions such as ideas, dreams, goals, visions, theories. We can also embrace such symbolic reflections and ideas to grow, develop, change, and react in response. We use symbols to express the non-material through language, artistic expression, and mathematic notation. Here we explore our capacity to express the non-material reality that guides us towards decisions and actions in the process of self-actualization. These ideas are certainly part of our reality, even in their immateriality, and are not held by any single belief system. They belong to us all.

For many Indigenous people, the notion of spirit is ubiquitous and applies to everything in the world, whether animate or inanimate. Given that the earth is a closed system, where physics tells us that all energy is not lost, and biology tells us that we, and our tables and chairs and pets, are all made of the same basic stuff, there is a veracity to this kind of animistic take on the world. (Don't we all yell at our computers from time to time?). Richard Wagamese (2008) shared this teaching on spirit in his book, *One Native Life*: "There is life-force in everything. Everything is alive, animate, moving and, even if we can't see that, we can learn to feel it. When we do, we come to true awareness of our ongoing state of relationship" (p. 161). The idea of spirit is also linked to the persistence of our ancestors in the spirit world. In that same volume, Wagamese offers another teaching that was shared with him by an Elder, that we are always being watched over and "guided and protected by our grandmothers and grandfathers in the Spirit World, our ancestors, the Old Ones, who love us regardless" (p. 146).

Here, in the East, we begin our journey around the Medicine Wheel. Regardless of which, if any, version of Spirit resonates with you, we hope you will find something here to connect with. Learning involves time and patience, and it requires the exploration of one's own identity. In our current fraught age, time often seems a luxury, but it is only over time that we can assess our learning and growth. So, be kind to yourself and keep in mind that it is not about how long it takes.

AUGUST ON THE SALISH SEA: TUCKED INTO A BAY

Miller: It was still dark when a sudden crack overhead jolted me awake. It was the boathook that had fallen from its perch and had come down hard on the boat deck above our cabin, right over my head. The scream of the wind, howling like a beast, wouldn't allow me to return to sleep. I pulled on my lifejacket and climbed out onto the deck into the elements. Through the moonlight, I could see the dim silhouette of the trees along the shore. The wind was blowing hard. We unzipped the overhead protective canvases from the enclosure to reduce the windage from the unintentional sail. I headed to the bow of the boat as my husband turned on the engines. We needed to release the anchor bridle and put out all 200 feet of chain, and then reattach the bridle to take the pressure off the windlass.[1] This meant that in the dark, and without any certainty, he drove us forward towards the chain, a few metres, in the hope that in doing so, I could release the full scope of our anchor chain, and yet in going forward in the dark we were not sure that we were staying in the centre of the channel. The shore was nearly impossible to see even with our strong bow lights. My heart thumped along with a matter-of-fact regularity. I executed my tasks, as did G. We secured ourselves and went below to make a pot of chamomile tea, listen to the wind, and watch the sky gradually lighten behind the trees with the early morning dawn. We returned to sleep when certain that we were not moving dangerously close to shore and that our anchor was doing its job.

Wind, it turns out, like a babe ready for birth, doesn't care how much you've slept, nor how 'ready' you are for your chore ahead. The East brings the present into focus, hyper-focus even. When attuned to the East, you are very much in the here and now (Lane et al.,1984). This point on the Medicine Wheel may be the beginning of the day, the beginning of life, a place of renewal and clarity. The East marks the spiritual element of being that tells you who you are even when no one is there to witness. In this quadrant, we are reminded to be open to possibilities, embrace the spontaneous, and trust. I take these learnings into my teaching practice to stay open, trust and take calculated risks.

So, what else did I learn from that early morning re-anchoring? I discovered that I am capable even in challenging conditions. I can remain

---

1 A windlass is a type of motorized winch to raise a boat's anchor.

calm amid a storm and trust my partner and easily communicate about all that is needed at that very moment. I also learned that when you know a storm is coming, you need to take down all possible canvases and put out all your chain before going to sleep. I also learned that there is very good holding on the bottom of that particular channel in the Copland Islands, even in a wind acceleration zone. As a teacher in a class, we need to remember the 'good holding' we have set our metaphorical anchors into and know that when the wind blows, we can remain safe with our students and ride out the storm.

Wind-time, sun-time, moon-time are just like a natural birth and death; even when predictable, they follow a rhythm all of their own. We can look at these as cycles, as a knowable span but with its own pace. Each spring, gardens are planted, with seedlings nurtured, placed into the ground according to recommended sowing times. These are not clock-times, but times related to typical weather patterns, sun, heat, rain for our region. Here in the Pacific Northwest, peas can be planted just after the last frost, when the soil is soft enough to work, whereas zucchini prefers a warmer soil (McDonald, 2014). Seeds sown in the ground take time to grow and develop their fruit. We know that we need to be patient and wait until the time is right and they have ripened and resist digging them up too early.

In their discussion of how an Indigenous student-teacher critiqued the classic junior science activity of growing bean plants from seeds as an experiment to determine the best growth conditions for them, Jones Brayboy and Maughan (2009) describe the student's incredulity that the bean seeds should be exposed to conditions that teachers know will see them fail to thrive. Indigenous knowledge systems see "the seed as alive and having purpose; it is not simply a 'thing' to be viewed but an active living object that 'does' things" (p. 12). When asked how she would approach the activity differently, the student-teacher, thinking of the same learning outcomes, described wanting to show students the changes in the night sky that indicate when it would be a good time to plant. The best location to plant would be determined by observing where these plants grew best naturally and the relationship of the plant to those around it. Her approach, in other words, was completely relational, including the relational responsibility she felt towards the care of that bean seed.

As an educator, a teacher, a mentor, what more can we glean from such insights? How can this inform curriculum and pedagogy? We ask readers to take a moment (or as long as you like) and consider your timeless learning if it's playing in your vegetable garden or making music. Reflect on learning about seasonal changes in the place you grew up – was there a rule about when to plant or harvest? Recall a scene that has been important for your learning or own teaching.

In the East, we are reminded that learning takes as long as it takes and involves patience, growth, and self-reflection. Our pedagogical approaches to curricula can reflect this if we move away from *delivering* curriculum, like delivering pizza, and closer to nurturing and growing a garden; it is done with love, effort, selflessness, risk, and reward. When we try to grow something new, we take a risk, learn about the plant, observe and nurture the growth, and tend to the plants as they develop new shoots, leaves, and fruit. This is also true when supporting others to grow and acknowledging that growth takes time; it is not limited to twenty minutes of *learning* in lesson plans delivered before a fifteen-minute recess of outside play. There is something about clock-time in our Western paradigm that limits our thinking to the concrete: yesterday, today, tomorrow; then, now, later is too ambiguous for many of us, and we seem to need greater precision. We feel more satisfied with *thirty minutes ago*; right now, it's 4:23; see you at 7:30. This is all justifiable, for sure, when our calendars are chalk-a-block full, and we *need* to know precisely when the next meeting is because others are counting on you, on me, on us, to be, and do all within an expected measure of time. After all, time is money. Right? But, yet during the pandemic, we heard from some of the youth closest to us that "time is fake."

Think of a good moment when the clocks, watches, and phones were away from you when the day lingered on as if extra hours had been slipped into your day for you to take in just that much more of your experience. Think about where you were and what you were doing. In moments of real learning, we may experience "flow" (Csikszentmihalyi, 1990). In these moments, we are, perhaps, our truest selves, in touch with the sacred within us, connected to all things.

The East is where the sun rises, and the day begins. East is where we grew up, with Saskatchewan being East of British Columbia and yet West of Manitoba. East, as in *East Van*, is home to many artists, artisans, awesome breweries. East is entirely relative. When we look out to the western horizon over the Pacific Ocean and know that the next land is Japan. Japan is to our west, but to others, say in Korea or China, it is to their east. What we're getting at here is that directions are relative, and one's positioning needs to be considered. In many Indigenous languages, the words for each direction are linked to geographic features and the sun's path. For example, cəlq̓ʷas describes the location of East Mall on UBC's Point Grey campus in Musqueam's language, hən̓q̓əmin̓əm̓. The word itself means to face inland, away from the water. These relational ways of thinking offer good insight into whether we tend to think in very Western or non-Western ways and what that might mean about how we understand the world.

One of the gifts of the East is presence, the ability to be here now and focus on this moment, connected to our place and time, to those around us and ourselves. Strong physical and emotional feelings help link us to the moment, yet we often turn to our technological devices as a synthetic substitute for actual connectedness. This hand-held addiction of permanent *connectedness* distracts from genuine bonds, reinforcing the fragmentation of our times. Think about what pulls us away from a task at hand, whether that be a news update about local politics, school openings and closures, election polls, the latest recommendations of managing during the pandemic, or just a text message that wakes a darkened screen to light. Think about what has recently interrupted you now from your reading, reflecting, and thinking. Then as a teacher, instructor, mentor, what are ways that you have experienced connectedness or fostered present awareness in your classroom? Is this a rare or common element in your practice?

As we weave together Slow and Indigenous pedagogies, we mark this as an important aspect of the decolonial project, rejecting the assumption of universalism inherent in Western philosophy (Weems, 2016). Further, holistic thinking and models are fundamental in achieving improved and more equitable outcomes for Indigenous students (Parent, 2011) and overall improved outcomes for *all* students. It does not, however, come without cautions. Ahenakew (2017) warns us against approaches to Indigenous education that are tokenistic and thus neutralize the inherently political act of including Indigenous knowledges or minimize the difficulty and discomfort in changing the way we work. For example, curriculum support documents such as *Shared Learnings* in British Columbia (2006) and *Weaving Ways* in Alberta (ARPDC, 2018) draw upon Indigenous expertise to inform their content but ultimately offer neutralized versions of lesson and unit ideas and pedagogies that fall short of the powerful potential that meaningful inclusion can create for learners. Curriculum documents created by the FNESC in BC, on the other hand, retain their power by focusing on specific curricular areas and grades (First Peoples English 10–12, for example, FNESC, 2018) and explicitly include the impacts of colonization and Christianity, rights, justice and rage, right alongside the more accessible stuff of relationships, generosity, spirituality, and storytelling. It may take more courage to work with Indigenous content in meaningful ways, but the yields are well worth the effort.

This is certainly part of the reason for our development of this book. In the East, we pay attention to the present – we are in the moment, attentive to our thoughts and actions – in a sense, it is in the East where we can take the kind of deep dive into a topic that Menzies and Newson (2007) call for. This deep dive, a dwelling with a topic, a project, an idea, can bring the diver to a place of flow (Csikszentmihalyi, 1990; Nakamura & Csikszentmihalyi, 2002). Although the idea of flow is multifaceted, the connection between slow and flow is with the individual's experience of a phenomenon where one is absorbed, body, mind, emotion – all is in harmony. This is both a subjective and integrated experience – in other words – it is holistic and present, thus perfectly suited for a concept rooted in the Eastern quadrant of the Medicine Wheel. This begs the question: what can we do to reconcile time conflicts to allow for a reasonable balance between work time and personal time and open up more possibilities for engaging in timeless time or flow, all the while attending to the here and now for ourselves and our students?

A clock is a non-living machine. Still, as we well know, we each have our internal clocks, the circadian rhythms of our waking and sleeping times. We age, like it or not, but we do, and we often mark this on an annual cycle with culturally informed traditions. Our children, or those around us, grow up, develop from infant to toddler, to child to tween, then adolescent and into adulthood. These transitions are populated by various lived experiences and abilities, every one of which is linked to years of age. As parents, caregivers, teachers, we nurture them along their journey, knowing that their journey, though not unique, is ultimately theirs. What we do to support their curiosity, learning, growth, and engagement to have rich and connected experiences is ultimately a question of pedagogy.

During the first six weeks of the COVID-19 pandemic in the spring of 2020, much of the world was forced to rapidly adjust to working from our homes.

> *Miller: In my house, I have a sixteen-year-old son on spring break and is now at school online. The first week following the holiday, and still a week before he'd connected with his teachers, he came home from a walk in our local forest park. He'd been curious about the life in the wetlands there, the creeks, and boggy areas, so he scooped a bucket of mud, sticks, leaves, and water and divided them into two two-litre jars and sealed them up to see if it would create a self-sustaining ecosystem. He'd already looked at water samples under his microscope and found numerous interesting, living and moving organisms. These jars now sit on the ledge in our front living room window. The silt has settled to the bottom of the jars, and bubbles routinely move around in the jars. He will check again in the coming weeks to see how things are when magnified. This is not a project to be rushed, nor to fit into a twenty-minute or even a one-hour block. It is entirely self-driven and responds to his own questions. I applauded his efforts and probed with questions, but he is driving his own learning.*

Here, in the Eastern quadrant of the Medicine Wheel, we are present, curious, connected, forgiving, and ultimately, not in a rush. What might that look like when we take these principles into a learning environment? This is where you as Reader come in – take a moment and imagine a day with your class at whatever age they are, at whatever stage of their learning journey they are, at whatever stage of your learning journey you are. Imagine taking a day that nurtures a project with multiple facets that extends all day. Imagine the potential for flow available in a day not chunked into twenty-minute consumable bits and siloed topics. Imagine the potential to cover all curricular areas with a day spent outside. Imagine the genuine respect for learning this would communicate to your students.

Our work in this quadrant is about connecting with the present, and one's inner-self, reflection, and self-reflection. This learning and growth is a process of tapping into our natural curiosity and encouraging our students to respond to theirs. Consider the following set of FPPoL and principles of Slow pedagogy as our part of our weavings within the East:

- Learning takes the time that it takes (FNESC,2008; Lipson, 2012; Holt, 2002; Payne & Wattchow, 2009),
- It is holistic and reflexive (FNESC, 2008),
- It is embedded in our memories, stories, and histories (*Aboriginal Worldviews*, British Columbia, 2015; FNESC, 2008),
- It is a process, at the moment, and requires attention, and patience (Lane et al., 1984; Lipson, 2012).

At this point of reflection, we ask you to reflect on what it was that spurred your interest in this work to teach and learn in a holistic way? Where have you experienced, witnessed decolonizing of curricula or pedagogy? (in or out of schools) What are the questions that emerge through your reading? Make a note of these in the book itself – there is space for you – make this conversation, not just one with us, but within yourself. What is *your* special purpose, and how can you ignite a curiosity for your students to find theirs? Here we return to the wisdom of Elder Gerry Oleman's (2019) teachings that finding our purpose is essential to our work as humans.

In the following chapter, after a short interlude, we move to the South, a place of emotion and feelings. Remember that these quadrants are not discrete quarters but porous, with the qualities of the previous designed to flow into the next – it is, after all, a holistic model. Keep in mind the spirit of the East as you move into the South.

DYEING THE YARN BEFORE THE WEAVE

It is not just the *what* of learning (curriculum) that makes this work exemplify Slow or Indigenous ways; it is the *why* (theory) and the *how* (pedagogy) of it. Why should we learn this material (whatever it is), and how do we go about learning it. Children (of all ages) are naturally curious, and by tapping into this natural curiosity, we can support them in their learning.

Here in between East and South, a southeastern moment as it were, we explore curricular opportunities that take up sentiments that have been laid out so far. To bring a new colour to our wool, we turn to natural dyes of our region, mindful of the season and what is ripe for the picking. In the Pacific Northwest, we have blackberries in the fall, along with salal berries, oak gals, black walnut, all sorts of lichen, cherry, and alder bark, and so much more. To gather materials for the dye pot, we take only what is needed, leaving the rest to the earth. Dyeing is not only a science but also an art that links to mathematics and business education as well.

To dye wool, in this case, the yarn that has been spun and wound into hanks or skeins, we need to scour the fibres with neutral pH detergent and pre-mordant them (with alum for wool and iron water for flax and cotton), so they can take up the dye into their fibres. This is a chemical process of slowly heating with an Orvus paste (a gentle detergent) in a very small quantity, and then pre-mordant with alum – potassium aluminium sulphate, which improves colour fastness for both washing and exposure to light. Some natural dyes have a built-in mordant (such as onion skins and lichens).

What is rather amazing about using natural dyes on natural fibres is that the colour that comes from some plant materials is not at first obvious. A lichen can be treated in a way that produces a pink or a purple, or a warm rust tone or brown. This is dependent on the dyeing process and whether it is heated, exposed to the sun, or fermented in an ammonia mixture.

Local Indigenous knowledge and practices can inform us about local dyes and textile practices. We can develop an appreciation of both current and historical practices.

The spirit of the East also connects with the unseen and one's own internal curiosity. Here, one's patience through the process relates to *slow*, the playfulness of the experiment, and the care of the mea-surements throughout the processes. We can engage in a multitude of learning opportunities as we bring together Slow and Indigenous ways of being and learning.

While elementary educators may be able to take up work such as this in ways that are naturally interdisciplinary, secondary teach-ers may find it easier to connect and collaborate with other teachers in themed learning that might extend across classes. For example, natural dyes can be cultivated in a school garden (black beans can be both a dye and food, as are beetroot, purple cabbage, and berries of all sorts), linking sustainability classes to foods, food sciences, biology, and chemistry. Chemistry classes may also look at the alkalinity and acidity of water and the impact they have on the colour. Mathematics education might concern itself with measuring the volume of water and weight of dry fibre prior to dyeing, along with the amount of dye matter, in order to establish a rich colour shift in the fibre – creating dye swatches of various gradients may also be of interest to arts and textiles teachers. There is much to explore in a class or outside with a solar oven dyeing materials.

In the next quadrant, the South, we remember our hearts, our emotions, our care.

5

South – Emotional – Relevance

Learning occurs most commonly in communities. We each need guides in our learning, those more experienced than ourselves who have done this work before, to show us the way. Teachers, Elders, other scholars, whether we speak with them in person or read their words on a page, offer this guidance. Watching, listening, reflecting, experimenting, improvising – these are our learning tools. The relationships that we build and nurture with our learning guides and the relationship we build with their ideas all support this work. Our learning is cumulative – we gather it bit by bit. It grows as both Archibald (2008) and Cajete (1994) suggest in concentric rings of relational knowing.

The Southern quadrant of the Medicine Wheel stands for the emotional aspects of our being in the world (figure 5.1). In this region, Lane et al. (1984) place the attributes of generosity, sensitivity to the feelings of others, noble passions, self-regulation, self-discipline, goal setting, discernment, artistic development and appreciation, love, loyalty, and the development of emotional intelligence (Gardner, 1983). While many of these attributes are not implicit in curricula, experienced educators know that emotional development forms part of the lived curriculum of everyday teaching through the establishment of respectful learning environments, attention to resolving social inequities and disputes, and self-regulation for task completion. Further, we know that nurturing the development

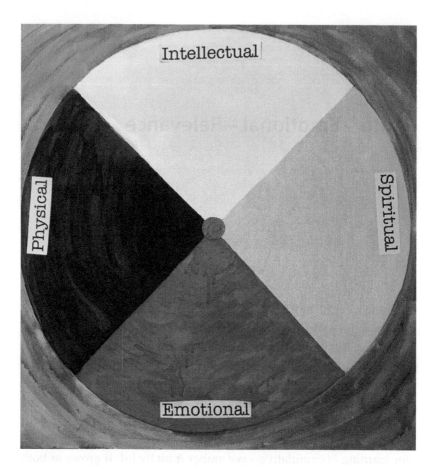

Figure 5.1. Medicine Wheel facing South, Emotional, Red.

Source: Courtesy of Shannon Leddy.

of any of these attributes lay in establishing trusting relationships, which is at the heart of our work in this quadrant. In this chapter, we look at the importance of emotion in education and how nurturing respectful relationships can support our efforts to build decolonial literacy as teachers to support our students better. We look at how trauma-informed pedagogy can support the development of strong and trusting relationships that lead to better learning outcomes. And we look at how Circle pedagogy can help us all find a way to work together.

WHY EMOTION MATTERS

Leddy: On a recent Vancouver morning, I drove for a short while behind a young man who had two well-known white supremacy symbols boldly displayed on the back of his car. The symbol, a sideways version of the circled thumb and forefinger that make the OK sign appeared on two stickers, one at either end of his bumper. Because much of my work is in anti-racist education, and I, therefore, keep up to date on such things, these stickers immediately drew my eye. Surprise, resignation, disbelief and sorrow whirled through my head and heart on a current of outrage. How dare he!? What nerve! Why, if I were his mother ...

As my anger settled in the face of its own impotence, I remembered what my job was, and a far more important question emerged. What was it this young man believed about himself and the world that would pull him into such a deliberately divisive philosophy? There was no doubt in my mind that if I or anyone else were to challenge him about either the prominence of this display or the ugly politics that underlie it, such a challenge would be met with anger, hostility, and possibly violence, as such responses are often rooted in pain and fear (Hurt People hurt people, as the saying goes), I wondered what types of experiences this young man may have had growing up to influence his thinking in this way. More importantly, I wondered, if I were his teacher, what could I do to call him in rather than calling him out? (I also wondered if he knew that particular symbol means anus in American Sign Language.)

Leaving our young man above aside for a moment, let's return to our overarching theme. One of the primary goals of Indigenous education, and all of the recent changes to Indigenize provincial curriculum, is to improve educational outcomes for Indigenous students. The reasons behind the disparity in educational outcomes between Indigenous and non-Indigenous students are well documented and thoroughly addressed elsewhere (Cote-Meek, 2015; King, 2012; Lowman & Barker, 2015; TRC, 2015b). As a direct result of those disparities, we insist it is crucial that Canadians appreciate the gravity and consequences of our collective history when it comes to the impacts of education. Not only were residential schools profoundly damaging to the relationships of many Indigenous peoples with school and schooling, but moreover, as we have discussed earlier in this work, the mainstream curriculum was designed to neutralize or erase Indigenous presence in order to maintain a colonial status quo. Therefore, part of our work in this text is to contribute to supporting teachers to support their Indigenous students.

The second goal of Indigenous education is to expand our educational practices beyond the grips of colonialist and Eurocentric narratives in both curriculum and pedagogy – this is the work of decolonizing our teaching. This means shifting the values of hetero-normativity and whiteness that have long dominated school curriculum to make space for the Indigenous pedagogies and ways of knowing that are inclusive, holistic, and that will improve outcomes for *all* students. We need classrooms that nourish the learning spirit, as Battiste (2013) has so aptly phrased it, nurture inclusivity, support the intellectual curiosity of learners, and build the emotional intelligence necessary for healthy maturation and keeping good relations. That is not to say we need to relinquish factuality and rigour, nor that we need to reject Western thinking. But it does mean learning to consider facts and rigour in holistic ways. It means we need to reframe siloed ways of thinking into interdisciplinary models that better reflect how we actually live in the world and how we might live better. It means we need to move away from anthropocentric ways of considering the world. It means owning up to the cognitive imperialism (Battiste, 2000) that has characterized education in this country since its inception and taking responsibility for decolonizing ourselves to work with students in empathetic and relational ways. It means, as Mi'kmaq Elders Murdena and Albert Marshall have phrased it, we need to work at *etuaptmumk* (two-eyed seeing; Hatcher et al., 2009). That is, we must encourage in ourselves the ability to see not just through a Western lens but through an Indigenous lens as well to get a clearer picture.

In this age of truth and reconciling, another point we want to offer here is that truth-telling does not only mean speaking about the historical impact of colonization, assimilation and genocide and their repercussions in our collective present. It also means shining light on the many vibrant, brilliant, and deeply engaged Indigenous people who continue to keep community knowledges and ceremonies alive. We need to celebrate the work of Elders, Knowledge Keepers, Artists, Parents, Teachers, Lawyers, Writers, Actors, Carvers, Tradespeople, Chefs, Beaders, Weavers, Hunters, Trappers, Fishers, Journalists,

Dancers, Singers and Activists, all of whom are symbols of Indigenous survivance (Vizenor, 2008), and many of whom are survivors of trauma and intergenerational trauma. We cannot shy away from the painful parts of our history, but we can balance our work by including our Indigenous peers in the present and lifting up the good work they are doing.

In our framing of this work, Indigenous educational practices embody this mandate, and Slow pedagogy invites us to take the time necessary to enact it. We work not to erase our differences but rather to find ways to work together across differences, build the dialogic capacities that form the heart of the community and the disposition of generous co-existence (Ingold, 2017). Again, it is all about relationships.

DECOLONIZING IS A SLOW AND CAREFUL BUSINESS

The young man in the story that opened this chapter presents some good fodder for considering the importance of including emotion in teaching and learning. Personal hard-wired traits aside, that young man *learned* his way of being in the world *slowly* over time. Just as we all have, so the undoing of all that learning, the troubling of deeply held assumptions and colonial frames of reference, will also take time, and of course, patience. Moreover, our work in this quadrant requires discernment and reflection to determine what serves us, what we need to build on, and what we need to leave behind. Our work, then, is to help our students understand themselves as emotional beings, understand their own reactions and responses, and build on those that serve us best, for example, using words to express frustration rather than lashing out physically. Since what constitutes "best" may vary and change over time, we need to help our students prepare for that too.

In 1994, bell hooks famously pointed out that education is never neutral, despite what we may have been encouraged to believe about it. Further, hooks notes the impact of normative narratives in curricula that have at their heart the maintenance of a colonialist agenda that routinely removes the body. This has included, in Canadian curricula, the promotion of historical narratives that legitimate European occupation and cultural domination, that erase or limit the inclusion of Indigenous voices and histories, that privilege whiteness, Western thought, philosophy and political systems, while ignoring issues of race, class, gender, and the thousand other intersectionalities that mark who each of us is. In other words, hooks is referring to what Battiste (2000) has called cognitive imperialism and its incumbent positivist assumption that there is *one* way of being in and seeing the world. Not only do we bring our own learnings and understandings as individuals to our work, but we also rely on materials that have been developed to promote particular perspectives. Who funds our textbooks? Who authors them? What were the historical and social conditions under which they were developed? The quadrant of emotion invites us to question neutrality, to leave it behind. It invites us to advocate for justice, examine our assumptions about ourselves and others, and transform our sense of what *is* into imagining what *could be.*

Unpacking these assumptions is often a slow process because it can be uncomfortable and even painful at times. So, the emotional quadrant of the wheel is also important because it makes space for us to forgive ourselves (and our own teachers) for mistakes made. It offers us space to find the courage to do better. The curriculum you were exposed to in your own school years was designed to blind you to the cruel impacts of colonization, to view Indigenous presence as unsightly or inconvenient or exclusively in the past. But it was conveyed to us by teachers, most of whom believed they were leading us down the best path because that is what they too were taught. They (again, most of them) did their work with love – the same love with which we teach our own students. It seems clear now that they were mistaken and that the materials they used were flawed. But rather than wasting our energy on being angry with the past, the Southern quadrant encourages us to nurture the courage required to repair those mistakes and to do better going forward.

> *Leddy: Perhaps you recall, as I fondly do, creating a diorama of an Indigenous village as part of your elementary school Social Studies curriculum. In fact, as a student teacher, I also remember giving this assignment to a Grade 9 class. It was the culminating activity in an Indigenous unit I developed that began with looking at contemporary Indigenous art and people and then traced each Nation's path back to pre-contact times, which was the curricular mandate I was meant to be fulfilling. As a beginning art and social studies teacher, this seemed like the perfect*

activity to me. They were learning about contemporary Indigenous peo-
ple and our history, but they were also learning about art and were given
the opportunity to create something with their own hands. For my part,
I wanted to offer my students the feeling of excitement I'd experienced
as a fourth-grader when I also got to make a diorama.

Andrea Sterzuk and Valerie Mulholland (2011) offer an example of how tacit aspects of cognitive imperialism manifest in seemingly innocent curricular activities, but which, on deeper consideration, reveal an underlying creepiness, to use their term. A diorama is a funny thing, rooted in the contextualist display theory of Franz Boas (Ames, 1994) and exemplified in many Natural History museums around the world. The diorama purports to offer us a glimpse into, in this case, Indigenous life, featuring a happy family scene from a faraway village, sometime long ago, rendered as static as a photograph. Ultimately, however, museum collections and displays were really about exhibiting imperial power and dominance over colonized lands and peoples. Creating a diorama in a school context replicates the cognitive imperialism that such displays represent (Sterzuk & Mulholland, 2011). In producing such a diorama, often made with craft supplies from home and populated with toy figurines, the authors assert that the "student is being socialized into the process of reinventing the imaginary past that discursively produces him as a member of the dominant class. The school is implicit in the process" (p. 25). In their concluding thoughts, the authors are careful to state that teachers *should* include Indigenous content and perspectives and voices in their curriculum but invite teachers to question why most of our curricular materials insist on focusing our attention on a pre-contact past.

Sharon Stein (2020), in discussing reconciliation in higher education, might refer to the diorama approach and similar curricular activities that may come to mind as a strategy of conditional inclusion. The inclusion of Indigenous content in the curriculum in the diorama example above does not involve the development of meaningful understandings about the history of colonization, genocide, and alienation. Rather, it is designed to pay lip service to inclusive pedagogies and non-Western world views while reifying the normativity of whiteness, Western culture's superiority, and the dominance of the positivist paradigm's idea of a single truth. It also traps Indigenous peoples in a romanticized ethnographic past where they are prevented from being understood as peers in our collective present. It checks a box, making things look good on the surface, but it reinforces the status quo nonetheless. Stein points out that this surface-level inclusion is often framed as a generous kindness for which Indigenous people should be grateful. Coming to grips with such implications regarding our own schooling and the schooling we offer our students can have a significant emotional impact on each of us, and we may experience shame, anger, regret, and avoidance. There is room for that in this quadrant. And there is room to move through those emotions to a place of healing and resolving to do better.

We know that many teachers worry about getting things wrong, making mistakes, not having enough background knowledge, and accidentally upsetting people (Dion, 2009). Grappling with that fear is part of our work in this quadrant. We all make mistakes. And there is increasingly more support for those who want to improve their knowledge to improve their practice. Perhaps this is why you are holding this book! We suggest spending time on your teacher's union's website to look for available resources that can help you peel back colonized curriculum in ways that are not tokenistic. Many faculties of education also have Indigenous education websites, as do many school districts. Buddy-up with a colleague and learn together! We recommend the work of Jo-ann Archibald, Robert Joseph, Leanne Betamasoke Simpson, Tanya Talaga, Drew Hayden Taylor, and Chelsea Vowel, each of whom will be of some help to you on your journey.

TAKING TRAUMA INTO ACCOUNT

When we first conceived of this text in the spring of 2019, we had no way of predicting the dramatic changes that would occur almost simultaneously around the world less than one year later in the face of a global pandemic, piggybacking as it was on the climate crisis, and culminating in massive uprisings in the name of anti-racism, opposing centuries of subjugation and violence against Black Americans. And although many Indigenous communities knew there were unmarked graves at former residential school sites, we could not have anticipated the heartbreaking discovery of 215 of them in Kamloops and the many more that followed. At that time, any consideration we gave to including discussions of trauma would have been limited to ensuring the well-being of Indigenous students and others, grappling with the impacts of potentially both personal and intergenerational trauma. Circumstances have changed, however, so it seems appropriate now to include a more fulsome discussion here.

Over the last few decades, there has been much written about the traumatic impacts of colonization on Indigenous peoples and increasingly of the potential for such trauma to resonate across generations. The Royal Commission on Aboriginal Peoples (1996), the TRC (2015a), and the National Inquiry into MMIWG (2019) have drawn our national attention to these issues in different ways. Educators, especially Indigenous educators, have been working hard to enact pedagogical approaches that take trauma into account and to create a curriculum that makes space for conversations about race, gender, class, and justice in the classroom in responsible, respectful, and productive ways. For Indigenous educators, this often involves heavy emotional labour.

In New Zealand, Maori professors Leonie Pihama and Linda Smith led a group of researchers in a project that looked at Maori approaches to trauma-informed care, drawing attention to the need for culturally informed approaches as well (Pihama et al., 2017). They note that, for Indigenous peoples, "trauma can be viewed as a contemporary manifestation of the succession of systematic assaults perpetuated through colonization and oppression" (p. 23). Moreover, they draw on a wide body of research while pointing out that traumas experienced by whole cultural groups, such as forced removal from traditional territories or slavery, reverberate over generations and may produce social conditions and behaviours that are then twisted into stereotypes and assumptions by those in the dominant culture group. Cultural safety then emerges as a key consideration in trauma-based approaches, especially when many of the people who provide health care and education *are* members of the dominant culture. This means that teachers need to engage in the kind of self-decolonizing work we are calling for here, examine our assumptions about Indigenous peoples, and question how they came to be. It also means that we need to learn about the specific cultures of our students and the specific culture(s) of the land on which they are teaching. More importantly, we need to recognize that we each see the world through the lenses of our own experiences and beliefs, and colonization is one of those lenses. Knowing that can help us shift the focus.

Currently, amid COVID-19, discussions of trauma-informed pedagogy must take a whole other set of factors into account as we suffer through financial insecurity, social isolation, the closure of schools, restaurants, hair salons, recreational facilities … the list goes on. Globally, people are stuck in countries they were only visiting, unable to return home on a flight or a cruise ship; families and communities have suffered a catastrophic number of deaths; first responders have been utterly overwhelmed and exhausted by the magnitude of it all (despite our nightly cheering for them banging our pots and pans, honking our horns); and all over the planet people are facing financial uncertainty, food scarcity, mental health impacts from social isolation, and the prospect of a very uncertain future. In Indigenous communities, the discovery at Kamloops and other IRS sites has been as salt on a raw wound. Especially in the face of global conditions that have made it hard to gather and heal together, the 2020s are off to an astonishingly rocky start.

Trauma is no longer something that happens to other people or happens only in the past. It has become a part of our daily lives. This pandemic has highlighted the divide of privilege even more between those who require public transport to get to and from service work (labour) and those of us who can work from the safety of our own homes, between those with job security and those whose gig economy work has suddenly dried up, between those whose pay reflects the actual value of their work, and those whose pay does not. In the same moment, violence against Black, Indigenous, and other racialized people, sparked by the death of George Floyd in Minneapolis on May 25, 2020, has finally enraged the broader public enough that massive protests have been taking place around the world, further highlighting cultural and racial tensions. We do this work in very volatile times, and many of our students come to us already, having suffered much.

In their 2015 article, "Practicing What We Teach," social work professors Janice Carello and Lisa Butler unpack the implication of primary and vicarious traumatization in social work practice and course work. Vicarious traumatization, their research revealed, is a "condition wherein exposure to information about the victimization of others results in emotional, cognitive, and other symptoms … that echo aspects of the victim's experience" (p. 263). These must be real considerations for the future of teaching. Drawing on the literature, they assert that effective trauma-informed practice considers teaching and practicing self-care, being judicious about exposing our students to depictions of violence and trauma through course materials, and acknowledging that we need to respond not only to students' intellects but to their emotions as well. We need to be aware of power imbalances, within our classrooms and our wider communities, so we need to help our students set healthy boundaries and build communities of care that will support their growth and well-being. We build on their work to suggest that this amounts to developing good and trusting relationships. And that, of course, takes time.

DEVELOPING EFFECTIVE PRACTICES

As we suggested earlier, the quadrants of the Medicine Wheel are not necessarily discreet segments, definitively separable. The boundaries between them are about as definite as the boundaries between seasons – there is always overlap. And perhaps this causes you some angst or frustration. Don't worry! The South is the perfect place to wrestle with that a little.

As part of our work together, we created a weaving workshop during which we produced an artifact with participants in the form of a felted and woven scarf. The other part of our workshop involves exploring how learning what is necessary to complete this task and working together to realize embodies key principles of Indigenous pedagogy and education. At the end of the workshop, we invite participants to place slips of paper containing the First Peoples Principles of Learning and Slow Stitch Manifesto lines (Lipson, 2012) onto the quadrants they seem to relate to. Participants often struggle to make a clear decision as to which quadrant each statement fits within. In part, this is because this approach is holistic, so each quadrant is necessarily interrelated. For those who have grown up within an exclusively Western ontology, this can present an intensely uncomfortable tension, as it seems to defy our attachment to certainty and to finding *the* right answer. Within an Indigenous ontology, there is an acceptance that nothing remains the same; nothing is fixed or permanent (Cajete,

2004; Fixico, 2003). Everything is always in flux. In many ways, the work we do in the South helps us grapple with such ambiguity and discomfort as we seek to discern, interrogate, and refine our values. It also helps us come to grips with humility as we realize that the world truly does not revolve around any one of us – we are in this together.

Our work in this quadrant is fundamentally about building good relationships and learning to discipline ourselves to be the best we can be in all aspects of our lives. It is a process, a stage in our growth and learning during which we build the skills we will need to enter into mature adulthood. Consider the following set of FPPoL and principles of Slow pedagogy, drawn together as our part of our summation on grappling with how to undertake the task of the South:

- It honours the art by which it is done (Lipson, 2012),
- It's not about technique (Lipson, 2012),
- Learning involves generational roles and responsibilities (FNESC, 2008),
- Learning is embedded in memory, history, and story (FNESC, 2008),
- Learning involves recognizing the consequences of one's actions (FNESC, 2008).

It is in this quadrant that the importance of understanding the interconnection of all things becomes apparent. Curricular silos satisfy Western thinking, but they also create a false idea that things are separable. Human understanding evolves over time through our connections to one another, through the stories carried by our families, and those we share with our friends. Nothing is really separate, and the South invites us to open our minds and hearts to that idea.

Leddy: In my teaching, to exemplify this, I often offer the example of baking a birthday cake for a party. If we were to look at this activity through a curricular lens, it is possible to make connections to every subject area currently covered in our schools. We might begin with planning the party and deciding who to invite (Social Studies, Psychology, Home Economics). We need to extend invitations to our prospective guests, determine a time to meet, and possibly provide instructions for how to arrive at the party (English Language Arts, Mathematics, Geography).

We would need to make a budget in order to plan for the party and ensure that there would be enough food and party supplies for each guest (Business Education, Mathematics). We would then get busy making the cake, which involves reading a recipe, measuring ingredients, and getting the cake baked (English Language Arts, Home Economics, Mathematics, Chemistry, Physics, Biology). Once the cake is baked, we would need to decorate it, and a truly elaborate cake might even require structural support (Fine Arts, Tech Ed). Finally, once our guests arrive and the party is underway, we might all sing Happy Birthday before the candles are blown out, and the cake is served (Social Studies, Home Economics, Music Education). Certainly, depending on the elaborateness of the party preparations, other aspects of the curriculum may arise as well, but from the example, you can see that we could potentially cover nearly every curricular area. But at no point during the process do we articulate the distinctions between those areas. They are seamlessly integrated as part of our daily lives.

CIRCLE PEDAGOGY

Settler scholar Robert Regnier (1994) wrote about the connections he observed between "process pedagogy" and his work with Indigenous students at an Indigenous-focused school in Saskatoon, where they regularly participated in a sharing circle as part of their school day. Looking to the work of Alfred Whitehead, who saw reality as evolving rather than fixed, Regnier theorized that the idea of evolution also applied to human learning and development, casting it as an ever-unfolding process and creating a clear link with Indigenous epistemology. He offers that human experience, much like reality itself, develops over time and is responsive to each new set of circumstances it encounters – the work of living is a process we each undertake daily. In his work with Indigenous educators in Saskatoon, he realized that an Indigenous Healing Circle is a form of process pedagogy (technically, of course, well predating either his or Whitehead's notions). In this context, the "curriculum" is formed through each participant in the circle (in this case, students, faculty, and all other staff), sharing their personal thoughts and feelings, the stuff of their lives. Because everyone at the school was expected to participate, there was a profoundly democratizing aspect to the process, where every person had the right to speak (or not, if they chose to pass) and the right to be heard.

As to the pedagogy, teachers accept as part of their work the responsibility to help their students discern their feelings and to acquire language that will help them express their thoughts in respectful and constructive ways. That is to say, circle pedagogy is a powerful tool in developing emotional intelligence, communication skills, community, and self-regulation. It is a form of co-constructed learning in which the students guide the learning by sharing their personal struggles and by listening to other members of the group for related stories and solutions. The role of the teacher is to nourish a learning environment of trust and care so that students feel secure enough to speak and mature enough to listen. Regnier (1994) expresses it aptly in stating: "in the circle, students belong to the stories and become the community that created them ... [as the] ... process moves them from silence to speaking, monologue to dialogue, isolation to participation" (p. 141).

In our own teaching practices, we have found circle pedagogy to be one of the most effective ways of creating community, honouring a democratic spirit, and calling students *in* rather than calling them out. We honour the emotional aspects of our students by making space for their emotions in the classroom and by modelling how to navigate them with community well-being in mind. This takes time. In the circumstance described by Regnier above, healing circles that involved the whole school were held once per week. In a classroom, it is possible to hold a circle daily. Another approach is to hold a circle only when an issue arises. In either case, the important part is that circle pedagogy is a process that unfolds over time and how participants create as they share in the process.

Whatever the frequency of these meetings might be in your teaching practice, there are a few keys to working effectively with this pedagogy: 1) understanding that the learning from the circle may be instantaneous in some ways, but it will also resonate over time; 2) framing this work as occurring within a brave space (rather than safe) empowers speakers to share, and reminds listeners of the courage it takes to speak from the heart; 3) the process takes as long as it takes, so enough time needs to be set aside that no one is rushed and so that everyone has at least one chance to speak.

As we wind down our time in the South, it is good to look back and see how far we have come. From dawn in the East, where we considered what it means to be fresh and new and to explore our values and ideals, we have come to the South where we learn to grapple with the impact of being alive in this place at this time. We have looked at what it means to nurture our spirits and our hearts, and those of our students. As we move into the West, we begin to think of the physical elements of the Medicine Wheel, of the well-being of our bodies, and the land we live upon.

WINDING THE WOOL

We began in the East, rounded the South, and now we face the West. Our hearts are in our work in this Southwestern moment, and we are well on our way. Winding our metaphorical yarn from a nicely dyed hank into a tight ball takes some work, and it is a step to not be skipped over, as to do so will result in a tangle of frustration. This is where we need a friend to hold the hank yarn in their hands, and from there, we can wind a centre-pull ball or a beautiful cake of yarn on our nostepinne (tapered stick for winding wool, shown in figure 5.2). This takes teamwork, time, planning and care. Here the careful winding of the work offers a moment of reflection and observation as the winding circles the ball larger and larger. The angle of the thread creates a pattern, brings order to chaos. This is the necessary prep-work to get our materials in order before the next step may begin.

We have used elements of sciences, mathematics, technology, and arts for curricular thinking. Here we look to Home Economics as a subject area to unpack in the past two quadrants as we build on each previous direction. The learning we tackle here considers the Spirit, that which cannot be seen, or the internal self, along with one's ideas, hopes, theories, and emotions. We can do this with any subject as we all have feelings about each area and the thoughts and hopes we develop along the learning path. The example of party planning illustrated in the previous chapter considers multiple subject areas and includes personal project planning, innovation, creativity, social engagement, and more.

This same kind of approach can be adapted for other areas of Home Economics: *why* is this important, *how* do we work together to see a

Figure 5.2. Yarn, ball, and tangle.
Source: Courtesy of Lorrie Miller.

final result, and *what* can we learn from such an exercise? This holistic approach to learning needn't abandon a central guiding subject area, like nutrition or meal planning. Still, it does recognize the complexity of lived learning and holds implications for creative thinking, local food supplies, social justice (who has access to quality food and who does not, why not, and does it need to be this way?). In the British Columbia curriculum, Family and Society 10 falls into this quite well with the big ideas addressing people's needs and wants along with problem-solving, "social ethical and sustainably considerations impact service design for individuals, families and groups" (British Columbia, Ministry of Education, 2019, p. 3). This also opens the conversation to what makes up a family and different family groupings and community structures. Our goal is to support relevant learning that is part of the growth of the child, of the learner. We do not bestow information or knowledge, but raise a caring and engaged community of learners. This can occur with any topic of investigation in a class, beginning with exploring the question: what do you care about learning, and who do you want to share your learning with? One way (and there are many ways) to tackle this is to tap into the students' natural curiosity. When students have the freedom to select a topic of investigation and inquiry, they are often intrinsically motivated to learn. When one teaches others about a topic that they care about, they too dig into the area further and learn more along the way. Here we suggest using both of these as ways to engage in learning and sharing this learning by way of peer teaching while caring about how one teaches others. By taking note of the audience (learners), students taking on a teaching role become more attentive or sensitive to those they are teaching. As teachers, we must always keep in mind that the *who* we are teaching is at the centre, not the *what*. We teach people *about* subjects.

6

West – Physical – Reciprocity

Here we are – three-quarters the way around the Medicine Wheel, in the West (figure 6.1) – where the sun sets, when the day cools, the frogs awaken, and the mosquitoes buzz about most annoyingly. Here we visit the West in our symbolic life's journey around the Medicine Wheel, connecting with our vision, intention, ourselves. When we look back at each of the previous directions and their attributes, and note that they are connected, not at all alienated one from the other. They are not siloed subjects. The West simply takes us deeper into the whole as in wholeness (not a dug hole). In the East, we explored the potential of the spiritual, the non-material world of ideas, in our work as teachers. In the South, we considered the role of emotions in our work as we became aware of how we felt about these non-material and material worlds. Now in the West, we engage with the physical, the material world, and consider, beyond merely moving our bodies, how we might work with our feelings and the non-material in relationship to this quadrant. This is a grounding into the physical, but with thought and presence. If we are as children in the East, and as youths in the South, we are invited into mature adulthood in the West. The West *is* all about action and movement, but not just for its own sake or for the sake of disciplining our bodies into fitness. Here we do the work of healing, of restoring balance in our lives. It is work we must all do together (Absolon, 2010).

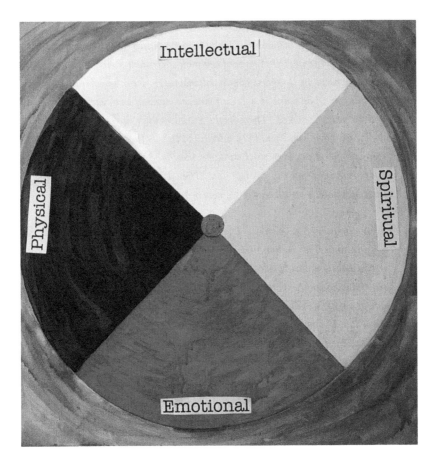

Figure 6.1. Medicine Wheel facing West, Physical, Black.

Source: Courtesy of Shannon Leddy.

Dear Reader, please take a moment now to pause and consider where you are – in the world at this moment of reading and consideration. What is your relationship to this place? Is this the location of your birth, the place of your choosing, or a place by necessity? Make a note to yourself – ground in the here and now, reflect on all that brought you to this moment.

> Miller: It's not a race; it's a journey. Be kind to yourself, and permit yourself to make a mistake and to grow." Sometimes I feel like a broken record when I say these things to the teacher candidates who

come into my office when things aren't going so well. I always try to frame the problem, whatever it is, as an opportunity to grow, reflect, and take up the next challenge. They own their next steps and their learning path. In the most conflicted instances, I ask them frankly, "Is this what you want to do? Can you see yourself as a teacher now and for years to come?" Then, in the end, it is their life path they are walking, and I want them to be mindful of this as they take their next steps. Sometimes the bravest students that have walked through my door were those who answered, 'no.' Then I listen as they consider their next steps an alternate trajectory to where they thought they were going.

In the early 1990s, when I was a new teacher in Pukatawagan, a fly-in-only Cree community in Manitoba, I took my southern and urban habits and attitudes with me to the distant North. The only road started at the train station and ended at the Northern Store where a half-cantaloupe cost $7.00 in 1990. The ice road didn't open until late December and only lasted until March if you were lucky. During the first week of school, I resumed my daily run, given that my exercise walking from the teacherage to the school was less than fifty metres.

"Ms. Miller." I heard a voice call from the side of the road. I stopped.

"Where are you running to?" Solomon asked.

"Nowhere," I answered.

"Then what's the hurry?"

I had no answer. But I laughed. He was, and is, right.

What is the hurry? As an art educator, program coordinator, and mom, I always struggle with this need to do and be all. I try to keep that naïve southern teacher, who was well out of her depth, close to my heart when I counsel these new teachers through difficult choices.

We have come to embrace Indigenous ways of knowing rooted in our early learning experiences through relationships with our Indigenous relatives and friends. Further, as new teachers in our differing contexts (one in rural Manitoba and one in an urban centre in British Columbia), as graduate students later on, and then as mothers. We have learned to recognize how education has worked to render our bodies, all bodies, invisible (hooks, 1994). We have learned to consider them only when they manifest in problematic ways through pain or illness (Shahjahan, 2015). In curriculum, bodies have been cast under the dominion of the mind in a manner much after Descartes' dualist philosophy, which sought to separate the two. In a further complication, curricula have also normalized some bodies while problematizing others. For decades, Indigenous and Black students and other People of Colour have been excluded from school curricula, affecting another form of invisibility and disconnection (Battiste, 2000, 2013; George & Dei, 1996).

We have come to Slow pedagogy later in life with the luxury of hindsight and patience, although slowing down is still sometimes a challenge. If you have ever tried to quilt by hand, or to clean and process raw wool, comb, card, spin, dye and weave new fibres into something new, or perhaps to master the old art of *tatting lace*, or maybe to embroider anything, then you know that slow is the only possible way. If you have ever rushed a class through a math unit before a test or rushed the lesson on safety basics in a Technology Education class, then you know that working too quickly can be disastrous and result in having to start over entirely – or worse. When Lorrie returned to her roots in art education, she found Elaine Lipson's *Slow Cloth Manifesto* (2012) spoke to her more about pedagogy than just about making in the material world. Lipson raises the importance of taking time to learn deeply, find the joy and beauty in your work, and honour the diversity of others and their stories, all as part of the textile-making process. She tells us that "Making things that take attention and care is not a waste of time; it's reclaiming time" (p. 9). We argue that raising realized educators takes care and attention, and it takes time. We bring our love of textile making, cooking, art making, and ceramics, very much grounded in the material world, to our roles as educators – these are all time-consuming activities if we want to do them well. We learned much of what we know about both art and teaching from others that we care about, grandparents, aunties, uncles, parents, teachers, and mentors, who showed us with their hands and stories of *how-to* and *why-to*. We see the approaches of Slow pedagogy and Indigenous ways of knowing as complementary fibres, the warp and the weft of a pedagogical cloth. We also recognize that Indigenous pedagogies, which are fundamentally learner-driven, align well with the culture of inquiry that has become an important component of modern educational practice. Where teaching is paced to correspond with learner readiness, learning is deeper and more meaningful.

THE UNSEEN

In the Western quadrant of the Medicine Wheel, the material world merges with the invisible as we acknowledge our bodies as containers for our spirits. The spiritual, unknown, dark, and mysterious notions are packed within us to be unpacked through reflection and ceremony. We are reminded that our body and mind are one and the same. Here the silos of subjectivity are melted down, forged anew; the sacred and spiritual are here for consideration. Here we turn to our inner conditions and our inner growth that is the lifelong process of becoming our true selves. We learn to see our bodies as more than mere mechanical containers for our minds. We are embodied beings, designed to be sensorial and experience a range of phenomena. In the West, we are invited to heal the disconnection between body and mind. We are material so that we may experience the immaterial.

The Sacred Tree (Lane et al., 1984) gives us the symbols of strength with both the bear and the turtle as they journey into the dark, one for hibernation, one for safety and one to shelter alone with oneself. Many of us claim that we simply have no time for an inner life. Yet, this is part of who we are as human beings. Think of a time when you allowed yourself to dwell in meditation, in reflection, in being that resulted in you feeling connected and replenished. How might you use this learning to enrich your teaching? Another question for you: do you find that you avoid inactivity, silence, or opportunities for reflection? Do you easily become bored from waiting, standing, or sitting without entertainment? When did you last truly "unplug"? Think for a few moments about why you chose to disconnect from your daily technology, or if you have not done this, ever, why not?

This is a good time to return to the notion of the holistic self, the very reason we are travelling the Medicine Wheel. In discussing the concept of Native science, Cajete (2004) draws on Husserl's phenomenology to point to the embodied nature of science learning in an Indigenous context, describing the notion of *lebenswelt* or lifeworld as a "vast ocean of direct human experience that lies below all cultural mediation, [that] forms a foundation of Native science" (p. 45). The precepts of phenomenology are rooted in our perceptions, our felt and sensed experience of the everyday world, and how we make sense of them. In Shannon's work with art inquiry, she frames this as noticing our noticing when dwelling with a work of art for an extended time. As we consider the physical element of the South here, we suggest doing a little phenomenological practice with your own body when it comes to the questions above and below. What are the sensory feelings you experience when you are engaged with technology? What are your sensations when you are not?

These are all questions we need to consider, both as people and, more importantly, as teachers. When have we supported our students with such moments of reflection, learning, being? How often do we pressure completion, resolution within a specified time? How often do we ask children struggling with attention how they are feeling in their bodies? Why? What are the other pressures or expectations of having all of this, or that within a specific time frame? What, ultimately, is our goal as educators? No rush to answer this – the replies will be varied as you grow throughout your career and life.

THE VISIBLE, PHYSICAL, MATERIAL WORLD

The materials, objects, things in our classes, homes, and world are valued in various ways. Certain things become more precious to us than others because we understand them as one of a kind, a rarity. Or we may have laboured to create them ourselves, so we are more aware of the time and energy invested in their production. However, in our modern fast-fashion-tech-upgrade-dollar-store world, we have also populated our lives with things that we view as less precious – items that offer only temporary joy or utility. In many ways, our purchases and accumulations have been, like our food, disconnected from the earthly materials of their production. Again, we have physical bodies that we can engage sensorially with our possessions. And our bodies are sustained by another great physicality – the land itself.

In the West, we are reminded of the ways in which our physical bodies come from the land. Through reflection and contemplation, we learn to understand ourselves as whole beings, and respect and care for our physical selves as part of our duty both to our holistic natures and our duty to the interconnected web of relationships that sustain us. As Michell (2018) notes, "the overall purpose of land-based education is to teach all humans how we are connected and interdependent with the natural world" (p. 17). The corporeality of our bodies is in constant interaction with the corporeality of all other bodies, including the Earth herself. We may sometimes forget that we have an equal responsibility to the land, as it is the provider of everything. We have the duty of reciprocity. If we were to love and respect the rivers and creeks throughout the world and value them and the homes they create for others, then we would not be pumping effluent from our textile industries into them, poisoning the creatures, plants and people downstream (Burgess, 2019). Perhaps we can learn how to resist temptations of having the newest phone, the latest fashion, the "better" whatever, and embrace *making-do* and learn how to appreciate the gifts we have. Imagine for a moment what might result from that?

Perhaps we lighten our footprint on the world, honouring Michell's (2018) assertion that "the land is considered a being that 'feels' when we walk on her" (p. 27). For Indigenous peoples, the notion of Mother Earth is not a metaphor. Making do with what we have can mean recognizing quality and nurturing interest in pursuing a design that factors in longevity, making quick and easy replacement no longer desirable. Throwing *away* an outworn item that has *no* purpose is an idea we are coming to reconsider in greater and greater numbers. We know now, through the work of such artists like Edward Burtynsky and his startling film, *Manufactured Landscapes* (2008), that there is no such place as "away." With some creativity, many used items can find a new purpose. Creativity is key to this process. Creativity, another non-count "thing" of value, must be nurtured and exercised. Creativity takes time, like that garden and seedlings we spoke of earlier in this book. As teachers, mentors, pedagogues, we must imagine our role in this changing world. Imagine the curriculum, pedagogy, the kinds of classrooms and other places of learning we can foster and influence.

This may sound much like work contained in critical place-based pedagogy (Graham, 2007) that challenges taken-for-granted notions of progress and our relationship with the land we inhabit and the systemic structures that shape that relationship. Michell (2018) explicitly discusses the key orientations that have shaped Western approaches to place-based learning, including positivism, constructivism, criticality and postmodernism. The West calls upon us to be critical of the lenses through which we have been taught to see the world. For example, a curriculum that includes discourses of environmental, ecological and sustainability education still uses language that evokes anthropocentric values. At its core, much of this work is underpinned by the idea of human dominance over the land, where the land is viewed as a resource for capital developments and/or as a recreational asset. Critical place-based pedagogy moves us closer to the Indigenous paradigm, where land is understood as the home for the matrix of beings and their interconnected relationships that populate the earth. No one being is more important than any other, and all relations should nurture respect and balance.

In particular, we need to consider this with the students under our care who have been alienated from their land, living in refuge (Miller et al., 2019). Linked to critical place-based pedagogy is a pedagogy of resilience (Miller et al., 2019), where teaching and learning in fragile zones seek to build actively engaged communities of learners, develop sustainability capacities, and foster values.

Miller's time machine: The skin of my fingers cracks near the nail, dried from frequent washing and hand-sanitizing gel. No amount of moisturizer undoes the drying impact. I am reminded of this as I sit at my wheel to spin fleece into yarn. It's an old-fashioned activity that has become my obsession. There is a real pleasure in transforming freshly shorn grass and soil imbued fleece. In this case, it is fleece from a Romney sheep raised on a family farm. Processing the fleece takes time, with careful soaking, cleaning and drying before combing it into a lovely fluffy nest ready to be spun. I like that all of this requires patience and adherence to a process where rushing results in matted and unusable material. I note the rhythm of the treadle under my socked feet as the fleece twists and pulls from my dry finger as it winds around the wooden bobbin. It will take days for me to fill the spool. At home, I blend my prepared wool with pre-dyed roving that I'd purchased from a local supplier. I am working on the yarn that I intend to weave on the loom that has a project nearly finished in my living room.

For me, spinning is a form of time travel; it connects me to people who came before me, before industrial levels of manufacturing. It also connects me with a community of local and international spinners. Though for a small group, the fibre arts are a growing passion as people seek out ways to make things for themselves, develop tactile skills, make by hand, and connect with the materiality of their lived experience. Salish weaver Debra Sparrow (1998) tells her story of reluctantly coming to weaving as part of a cultural revival project. She is now known widely for her impactful artworks and for her teaching others this living tradition.

Working with wool is a multi-sensory experience with the feel of the fleece, the yarn in my hands, the lanolin on my skin, the full fragrance in my nose, and the planning of the next steps in my artworks and crafts.

IN THE CLASSROOM

In the classroom, whether that is actually in a school, or outside in a park, or the wild, we look to examples teachers can draw upon for their inspiration. In our region of Canada, our curriculum for K–12 learners is organized into "big ideas" that frame subject areas. This lends itself well to the pedagogic cloth we propose woven from Slow and Indigenous ways of knowing. Curiosity is encouraged, with the freedom to explore ideas and our lived world. A starting point for a learning unit might be on *ways to understand our neighbourhood*. In the West, we are looking at our lived experience – and so walking, riding, biking through the local area and then carefully noting the environment, the sights, sounds, smells, the way the area is arranged. Questions to consider: Who lives here now, are there trees, what kind are they and how did they come to be there, were they wild trees or planted by city workers. What birds, insects, animals share this neighbourhood with you? What are some stories you know about this neighbourhood? Who might you ask to learn more about the stories of this area? What are your feelings about this area? Do you have favourite spots to go, play, explore?

PEDAGOGY THAT NURTURES

This all has a feeling of goodness, of aliveness. So, how does a pedagogy, or a curriculum, add to our sense of wholeness and connectedness, feed our soul, energize our spirit … however one chooses to phrase this? Remember that curriculum is the *what* and pedagogy is the *how* of teaching and learning. In the West, we are called to deep contemplation to still the mind through connecting deeply with our bodies. From this practice can emerge pedagogies designed to keep our students connected to the earth and the materiality of our bodies and us. We require our bodies to help us learn, with our senses, and our mobility. We gather materials we will need and consider what we can offer in return for them. We may source things close to where we are, or from far, faraway, knowing that every such transaction has some kind of cost (Burgess, 2019). Therefore, we must treat our materials and ourselves with care and respect, again knowing that all of this is interconnected, and we and our making are just one small part. We connect this concept to Lipson's (2012) Slow Cloth manifesto; we can look beyond the textile into a broader material world:

- It honours the thing it makes and the user of the made thing,
- It honours the place where it is done,
- It's an ethic of working with textiles and cloth,
- There are no instructions,
- It honours the source of the materials (Lipson, 2012).

Curriculum matters – this is the *what* of learning (even if it includes actions of how) when students are connected to the learning content when they can see themselves and their experiences in what they read, do and learn in school, then they care. It becomes meaningful learning (Miller, 1995).

Perhaps this is where Lane et al.'s (1984) code of ethics comes in. We need a curriculum that includes Indigenous ways of knowing in line with holistic ways of being in the world. The Eurocentric belief system prevalent in curricula has tended to hold close to modernist ideals, positivist *truths*, and faith in capitalism (Battiste, 2000; Donald, 2019; Michell, 2018). We need pedagogies that nurture questions about finding a balance between objectivism (if this even exists) and subjectivism, between individualism and collectivism.

As educators, we are familiar with the importance of creating a positive and supportive classroom environment that allows or encourages spaces for learning. Our work is to guide our students to the possibility of growing towards their full potential. If we also practice authentic gratitude and *respect* in the breadth of its meaning, then we can further support these learners along their journey of growth and self-actualization.

RELATIONAL PLACE-CONSCIOUS PEDAGOGY

Most folks raised in Judeo-Christian traditions have grown up with that well-worn line from Genesis that gave *man* "dominion over the fish of the sea and over the birds of the heavens and over the livestock and over all the earth and over every creeping thing that creeps on the earth" (Genesis 1:26). Many other traditions and cultures hold similar views, the gist of which is that the earth belongs to us, that it is something we can own, manipulate, and extract from freely without concern for consequence. It is literally, in some of these traditions, our God-given right. In the West, we reconsider this position and offer that the land does not belong to us, but rather we belong to the land. In the teachings of many Indigenous Nations, we are reminded that we borrow the land from our children, and we are asked to think of our actions in the context of their impact for the next seven generations. We wonder what things would look like globally if CEOs, managers, and board members of some multi-national companies had been raised to consider the world, resources, and inhabitants in this way. Would they have designed product obsolescence and continued extraction and dumping practices? What would their bottom line be with such a world view? Similarly, Slow pedagogy encourages practices that help us reconnect to our senses, re-inhabit our bodies, and understand them as our interface with the world, with the land, and aims to draw our consciousness to deeper understanding by drawing on more than merely our thinking. Slow pedagogy nurtures the kind of wisdom that comes from *doing* (Payne & Wattchow, 2009). We are a part of this place, not separate from nature, but are connected to all our relations (other than human beings). Herman Michell (2018) tells us that "[d]ifferent relationships and perspectives exist in relation to the land that need to be exposed, challenged interrogated and replaced" (p. 10). Here we aim to be a part of that interrogation and offer additional guidance and hope to educators.

Under the stars, in the forest, at the edge of the sea; for many, these places hold special meaning; for others, they may even be sacred. Too often, though, these places on the land and beneath the waters are viewed as commodities, whether individually or corporate-owned property. This poses numerous challenges, many of which have risen to a crisis level over the past hundred or so years. Biologist, poet, writer, mother, educator, and Citizen of the Potowatomi Nation, Robin Wall-Kimmerer (2013), asks "[h]ow, in our modern world, can we find our way to understand the earth as a gift again, to make our relations with the world sacred again?" (p. 26). She focuses on the impact of science on Western ways of seeing and feeling about the world. She tells us that science is good at helping us know more about our world, but it does little to allow us to care more about it. Science may allow us to see in smaller, more refined detail, or across greater distances, but can it actually aid one in seeing the sacred, or "does it bend light in such a way that it obscures it?" (p. 345). We recognize that these locations are home to plants, animals, and people. We are all related.

Learning is relational; it is always relational, whether through one's relationship with oneself, the subject matter, or one's teacher or mentor. When that relationship is positive, the learner feels respected; trust is built and then meaningful learning can happen. We are reminded again of Goulet and Goulet's (2014) attention to the relational considerations of an effective teacher. Learning is lived and storied. We need to remember to listen carefully to the stories of others and learn how to share stories of our own. Further, Indigenous knowledge is not a single concept, and so curriculum and pedagogy must take into account Indigenous diversity and local diversity of Indigenous knowledges (Battiste, 2013).

The work we are called upon to do in the West is challenging. Just as the Western quadrant represents the era of mature adulthood in our life cycle, we also find many of the challenges that adulthood can bring. Surmounting these challenges requires reflection, contemplation, self-discipline, self-regulation, and perseverance. In addition to the work we must do to renew our respectful relations with the land, we need to nurture respectful relations with our bodies and lead our students to do the same. We need to give back – to transform our learning into lessons we can share with our students to nurture and ensure our collective well-being. We need to think about what the seven generations before us have left for us, and, more importantly, we need to think of what *we* will leave for the seven generations ahead.

When we began in the East, learning about weaving was a metaphor for the work we do together. For many, it was an abstraction that offered little more than a glimmer of illumination. When we hear words describe something new for the first time, the words themselves are symbolic, gaining meaning only as we remain patient, observant and engaged. In the South, we open to the heart – the emotion, the feelings associated with this new learning. Perhaps excitement becomes frustration, only to suddenly transform into understanding. We attend to the physical in the West – feeling, seeing, trying, making, and repeating the skills. We discuss and analyze the making, ask questions, explore, and return to the abstract … the *what-ifs* of teaching and learning. Abstractions transform into concrete understandings as we learn to feel our learning with our spirits, with our emotions and with our bodies. Our work on the Medicine Wheel is not yet complete. We have yet to attend to our minds.

SETTING UP THE LOOM

There are many, many different types of looms that come from a variety of traditions. But in each case, the warp threads are organized, measured, and fastened to the frame of the loom or across and through the heddle. These warp threads, counted and organized depending on the diameter of the thread themselves, are meticulously laid out so that they do not tangle and ensure they are sufficient for the project and not too tightly crammed to weave the weft of the same material.

The weaving tools are many, both mechanical and analogue, complex and simple, all depending on the tradition the weaver is drawing from. The Jacquard Loom inspired the first computer language with punch cards indicating the pattern of the weave. This is a natural fit with computer science, history, cultural studies, anthropology, art, textile studies, and mathematics curricula. Yet, even the work of any weaving practice requires a framework, whether that be a rigid heddle loom, a pin-loom, a back-strap loom, Inkle loom (the list goes on) or if it is basket work, the foundational spokes that orient the rest of the weaving. To weave anything, one requires a structure, an organizing tool, a frame.

Here, following the third quadrant of our journey around the Medicine Wheel, we have been reminded of our material world, the physicality of our every day. We encourage you to keep in mind that the invisible is very real; thoughts, feelings, ideas, emotions, hopes, and curiosities are all just as tangible as the mathematic manipulatives, the lunch boxes, the art and craft supplies, all the *things* of our classrooms. In the next section, we address the mind, the intellectual and thinking quadrant, again an invisible arena. It is often the realm we start within our schooling activities, but it need not be. What might things look like if we begin our learning exploration with what we care about, what we hope for, or are deeply curious about?

7

North – Intellectual – Responsibility

Winter days are good days to stay warm inside, maybe weave or bake some bread, and think about what North means. North (figure 7.1) represents the mental, the intellectual. In our journey around the Medicine Wheel, it is the final stop (at least before the next round starts). Since we are writing for teachers, it may have seemed like the logical place to begin because here in the zone of the intellect is where we often place the locus of our work, the thinking and planning portions that carry us through each year. But we honour the teachings by following them around the Medicine Wheel, from beginning in the East and ending in the North. Let's recap for a moment at where we have been before we take stock of where we are now. In the East – the beginning of the journey, the start of the day, connecting with the present and one's spirit, the intangible. From there, we walked to the South – where we connected with emotions, the uplifting, the heavy and all in between. Following, we entered into the Western realm where the physical, the material world dominates and connects us with our feelings and sense of being. Recall that these are not truly in existence in isolation, but instead they are integrated throughout. To be, feel, and do, and now this is where we analyze and reflect. What does all of this mean? Here in the North, we settle into a place of wisdom, humility, reflection, and analysis.

In this chapter, we wish to pull at the deceptively simple-seeming nature of this quadrant and explore aspects of mental activity beyond

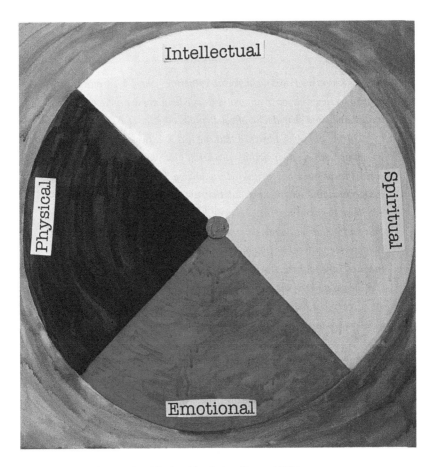

Figure 7.1. Medicine Wheel facing North, Intellectual, White.

Source: Courtesy of Shannon Leddy.

mere thinking. Lane et al. (1984) offer a fairly long list of capacities held in the gifts of the North: synthesizing, predicting, discriminating, imagining, analyzing, calculating, remembering and interpreting are just a few of the functions they include. They also discuss the notion of volition and fulfilment as belonging in this quadrant, as well as the notion of detachment and of balance. Perhaps most importantly, however, the North encourages us to see how all things fit together – beyond synthesis; this means recognizing the interconnection of all things and ideas and creating interdisciplinary learning opportunities that make space for students to see those connections as well.

Leddy: Recently, I was at a social gathering where I encountered a woman, perhaps closer to my mother's age than my own. We connected immediately and shared a lot of good laughs over the course of the evening. During our chat, I learned that she was a sixties-scoop baby who'd grown up with her own siblings in a strict protestant household. At one point, the conversation turned to terminology. I had been using the word Indigenous, and she pointed out that we are all Indigenous to somewhere, so the word has little power. She told us that she preferred to be called an Indian, although she was quick to add that she didn't really feel comfortable with other Indians. "The difference between me and other Indians," she told me, "is that I know it as the William Tell Overture, and they know it as the Lone Ranger theme." Conscious that it was not my place to challenge this perception, I let the moment ride, giving her idea some space.

Sharing this story provides a moment to reflect on some of the key concepts that underpinned her thinking. First and foremost, it draws attention to some of the fundamental tropes of colonizing education. The speaker rejected her Indigenous identity, revealing her assumption that Indigeneity was necessarily equated with ignorance. In this way, she also reified notions of high and low culture that placed more value on Eurocentric aesthetics and norms, elevating them to the category of high culture. The underlying assumption is that pop or low culture was for the uneducated. But she did not come to this implicit bias on her own. As teachers, educators, mentors at any level of teaching, we need to be first aware of our own biases and also to support our learners to unpeel their own bias-onion.

WHAT COUNTS AS KNOWLEDGE? HOW MUCH KNOWLEDGE COUNTS?

The story above illustrates two key elements of colonized thinking, although there are arguably more potentially at play. The first of these is what Susan Dion (2007) calls "perfect stranger" positioning. Dion suggests that our relationships with Indigenous peoples are rooted in "what [we] know, what [we] do not know, and what [we] refuse to know" (p. 331) about Indigenous peoples. When allowed to remain static and unexamined, our frames of reference can deliberately preclude acknowledging these relationships. In many ways, these disconnections rest in our subconscious, sitting in pools of unexamined stereotypes, topping our lists of avoidances. This positioning is not exclusive to the context of Indigenous/settler relations in Canada and can manifest in any cultural or social dynamic where tension exists. In our current educational context, however, especially with ever-increasing expectations for teachers and their students to grapple with decolonized/decolonizing curriculum, we cannot move forward together as long as that positioning remains static. This is the realm of the mental/intellectual, the North.

The second element at play falls under the rubric of what Marie Battiste (1998) has termed "cognitive imperialism," which expresses a distinction between what kind of knowledge counts and what does not, determining the dissemination and evaluation of such through an exclusively Eurocentric lens. In a country where the federal government deliberately acted to inflict both physical and cultural genocide against Indigenous peoples (Coulthard, 2014; King, 2012), it is little wonder that their treatment within curricula was biased, historicized or excluded. How can one learn to respect a knowledge system that is deliberately suppressed? How can one build relationships with those they have been taught not to see or not to see clearly? This is also the realm of the North, where analysis and critique of dominant structures of knowing to make space for Indigenous knowledge systems and ways of being.

In critiquing a recent curricular overhaul in Alberta, Dwayne Donald gets to the heart of how curricula have been historically approached through a distinctly Western lens. Framing curriculum development as an exercise in citizenship, he notes, "the kinds of citizens that adults have in mind derive from orthodox, epistemic assumptions that are often characterized as common sense" (p.106). His critique, of course, points to the difference in Indigenous and Western ontologies and the colonial assumption that one is necessarily better than the other. While we know as teacher educators that things are changing, and this stranglehold is no longer as tight as it was, the tension is also not yet resolved.

IT REALLY ISN'T ABOUT THE LESSON PLANS

Before we look at what a holistic version of intellect can mean in an Indigenous framework, we need to lay some further notions aside. In every class I have ever taught about Indigenous education, students express the need for lesson plans at the beginning of the course, despite my assuring them that I wouldn't be supplying any. By the end of the term, many of those same students feel confident leaving the course without one, while others still report their disappointment at not receiving prepared lesson plans. But receiving and applying a lesson plan that has been created by someone else does not equate to engaging in Indigenous education. Including an Indigenous resource in a lesson is an important beginning to work with Indigenous students and Indigenous content. However, *meaningfully* including an Indigenous resource into your lesson and using it well requires a little more. Teaching in a *good way* requires us to engage in the process of decolonizing ourselves first, of detecting and interrogating colonial frames of reference that have enabled personal, cultural and institutional bias. Teaching in a good way requires us to do some unlearning and relearning. It requires work.

The North asks us to examine not just the contents of our work but our pedagogy as well. It asks us to consider our relationships, to question our frames of reference, to de-centre ourselves, and question our notions of assessment. It asks us to be flexible in our thinking, to become teacher-as-student and allow our students to be as teachers (Freire, 1970). It asks us to shed our perfect-stranger cloak, remove the shawl of cognitive imperialism, and try seeing with two-eyes (Bartlett et al., 2012) by adding an Indigenous lens to accustomed Western ways of seeing. This means that as teachers, we are asked, and need to be open to, collaborating across disciplines, creating project-based learning that touches on multiple aspects of the curriculum, and providing multiple points of entry into learning for each student.

This work may not always be easy. De Leeuw et al. (2013) point to the fact that reconciliation efforts designed as decolonizing practices that support the hiring of Indigenous scholars actually function to perpetuate conquest/colonial violence by placing the burden of re-education back on Indigenous peoples. This, of course, also applies to teachers, staff, and administrators within school districts. That is an important consideration as teachers begin to embark on the path of trying to build relationships with their Indigenous colleagues. Teachers need to take on the burden of reconsidering assumptions and frames of reference themselves. It is okay to ask for support from Indigenous colleagues, but it is also okay for them to say no. This chapter, grounded in the realm of the intellect, of knowledge and wisdom, requires us to trouble the colonized nature of mainstream culture and to render uncomfortable the notion of what *counts* as knowledge. But don't worry! We're here to help!

ADDING AN INDIGENOUS LENS

Ultimately, our work as teachers is about imagining how the world could be and creating lessons, strategies and school environments that support that vision through student learning and engagement. Basically, we are doing it for the kids – and kids are designed to grow. Therefore, learning is not a project in the sense of one-off making; rather, it is a lifelong process that begins with reflection and conversation, with the slow acquisition of skills through apprenticeship and observation, rooted in the needful daily realities in the places we exist. Let us now explore what we *do* mean when we refer to the mental or intellectual.

Because of the ontological differences between Indigenous and Western ways-of-knowing (see chapter 1), it is not easy to find an easily translatable theory of learning that might encompass both. Perhaps the closest theory, though, is that of Social Constructivism. Associated with the work of Jean Piaget and Liev Vygotsky, this theory of learning views experience as rhizomatic – spreading out in all of the directions of a child's lived experience (Watson, 2001). It is student-centred and seeks to create learning experiences that are contextual, building upon what is already known and understood to scaffold up to higher levels of learning and thinking, like the concentric circles of learning and knowing described by Archibald (2008) and Cajete (1994). As we illustrate in the following paragraphs, much of this is resonant with Indigenous teaching and learning, but an important difference in this philosophy is linked to the educational outcomes desired during the time of its conception. That is, social constructivism is theorized on the basis of an educational system that sought to turn out a homogenous work-ready citizenry that would carry on with the needs and concerns of modernity and capitalism. It is fundamentally anthropocentric and concerned mainly with the goals of nation-building.

Indigenous education shares many of the same characteristics as social constructivism in that it is student-centred and seeks to build on prior learning towards ever more complex skill sets and understandings that are rooted in the context of students' and teachers' lives (Cajete, 1994). Unlike its theoretical cousin, however, it concerns itself first and foremost in "a sacred view of Nature … [with] … integration and interconnectedness [as] universal traits of its contexts and processes … [where] … teaching and learning radiate in concentric rings of process and relationship … [that] … adhere to the principle of mutual reciprocity between humans and all other things" (p. 29). This way of theorizing teaching and learning seeks not homogeneity of learning outcomes but rather honours that each person is special, with special gifts to offer the community, that should be nurtured in a lifelong process of learning.

It is easy to see the parallels between these two ways of thinking, and it is worth exploring how we might work towards uniting them for the benefit of all of our students. One way of doing this is to employ etuaptmumk (two-eyed seeing), as previously mentioned (Bartlett et al., 2012). This concept came to the fore recently through Miq'maq Elders Murdena and Albert Marshall in their work with Indigenous science educators at Cape Breton University. There is also an excellent TEDx talk by Rebecca Thomas that discusses this concept in a very accessible way and ends with a powerful spoken word poem (Thomas, 2016). Essentially, etuaptmumk means seeing the world with one eye through the best that Western ways of thinking and knowing have to offer and seeing the world with our other eye through the best that Indigenous ways of thinking and knowing have to offer. An example might be exploring the colonial perspective that the areas west of Lower Canada were unoccupied and barren, versus the Indigenous perspective that they were indeed occupied and abundant with resources if you know where to look. Together, those two versions of reality make up a complete picture. Of course, this doesn't happen all at once. It requires the same kind of patient exploration of new ideas and concepts that we offer our students. To truly see with two eyes requires an unpacking of our old assumptions about knowledge and knowing, a re-shaping of our frames of reference, repositioning ourselves as learners always first. We need to clear the colonial film from that Western eye. Does it seem like we are talking in a circle? We hope so … that's how it starts.

DEVELOPING EFFECTIVE PRACTICES

At the start of this chapter, we pointed out that the gifts of the North include synthesizing, predicting, discriminating, imagining, analyzing, calculating, remembering, and interpreting. Consider the following points from FPPoL and Slow pedagogy, as found in Elaine Lipson's 2012, *Slow Cloth Manifesto*, that we have drawn together as our part of our summation on grappling with how to undertake the task of the North:

- Learning is holistic, reflexive, reflective, experiential, and relational (focused on connectedness, reciprocal relationships, and a sense of place; FNESC, 2008),
- It's a mission statement and a set of values for making with meaning (Lipson, 2012),
- It's a conversation about process and practice, sustainability and skill, beauty and expression (Lipson, 2012),
- Learning recognizes the role of Indigenous knowledge (FNESC, 2008),
- It's not a project (Lipson, 2012).

Synthesizing what we have described over the course of this chapter, we want to highlight the importance of relationships to this work: relationships with our students as unique individuals; relationships to the land where we do our work; relationships between ideas across curricular areas; and relationships to building the skills that living a good life requires. So the work of the North is to build our own knowledge and skills in ways that support and nurture these many relationships. It is fundamentally interdisciplinary in nature.

Below we offer three examples of the way in which such work might be approached by offering and building upon a few good projects we have come across in our research. Rather than providing unit plans, we describe each project briefly, along with the curricular areas it covers. In cases where we were able to make further interdisciplinary connections, we offer those too.

Kendomang Zhagodenamonon Lodge

In January 2020, Caroline Alphonso, the education editor for *The Globe and Mail*, published an article about Thunder Bay teacher Melissa Roberts, who worked with her school District, community Elders, and the local friendship Centre in a program designed to help at-risk students complete credit requirements for graduation across the curriculum through bringing Indigenous knowledge and skills into her classroom. Together they created the Kendomang Zhagodenamonon Lodge project that brought students together with Elders in order to work on deer hides donated by local hunters. Then over the course of the school year, working with the guidance of both their teacher and community Elders, students scraped, tanned, and smoked the hides, eventually turning them into medicine pouches. Through this work, they were able to gain credits in English for their writing about the process, in math for the measurement required in creating stretcher frames, and chemistry in considering the role of acids and fat in softening hides with deer brains.

We found this such a gratifying story to read as it gets to the heart of what the gifts of the North can help us do. While we recognize that a year-long hunting and processing unit is not a possibility for most teachers, we think that the creativity and flexibility demonstrated by the educational stakeholders, in this case, are exemplary. In urban contexts, teachers may turn to smaller-scaled land-conscious projects to facilitate holistic and cross-curricular learning such as building and nurturing gardens, building bat boxes or birdhouses, initiating and engaging in beach and riverside clean-up and reclamation projects that revitalize salmon streams. Each of these examples offers multiple curricular affordances that connect learners to land.

As schoolteachers, we have come from a tradition of subject-focused learning. We have often treated social studies, mathematics, science, art, physical education, music and so on as discrete subjects to be taught, practiced, and understood in their own singular context.

Yet, we now know that these are related areas of learning. To know about and to understand a topic, we need to engage with that topic in multiple ways. These are not strictly objective topics to be learned only through our intellect; they are grounded in history, in our lived experiences, and felt in our curiosity, apprehension, and even in our surprise of discovery. By attending to our students truly in a holistic way, as called for by many educators and scholars and guided by the pedagogies we put forward here, we can support our students to grow and not be afraid of the challenges before them. The examples we present from Indigenous contexts are an illustration of how this wholeness can be attended to.

Button Blankets and Starblankets

We know that globally, all Indigenous groups have used, and some continue to use, local materials to make clothing, bedding, and housewares. With the introduction of and trade for Western materials, such as pre-felted wool and bolts of printed cotton fabric and silk ribbons, many communities developed new traditions and innovations as a response. For instance, on the Northwest Coast of British Columbia, many communities create button blankets that employ the distinct non-Euclidian geometry of Northwest Coast design, often a vibrant red or stark white, imposed on a black felted or fabric background and fringed by abalone and other shell buttons to stunning results.

On the prairies, many Nations adopted quilting techniques that worked well with traditional geometric beadwork patterns to create the Starblankets that are now an established part of a ceremonial tradition in some contexts. FNESC created a unit within their (now retired) First Peoples Math 9 curriculum document for learning through the creation of button blankets, which learning is equally applicable to the creation of a Starblanket quilt. While the majority of learning in this project is rooted in the BC math curriculum, specifically for Grade 9 learners, there is no reason that a unit like this could not be done with students of any grade. Further, besides math, there are opportunities here for teaching and learning within Arts education, Social Studies, English Language Arts, Technical education, and Home Economics education, just for a start, and if one truly wishes to engage in a cross-disciplinary and integrated approach to learning, then we can look deeper at the threads that connect each of the subject areas listed and more. Such a unit requires community connections and the building of relationships with Indigenous school district personnel and local community members. Finally, such a project need not be a class-wide collective project but could also result in a small artifact of learning created by each individual student – the possibilities here are endless.

Tiny Orange Sweater Project

In the summer of 2021, just a few months after the discovery at the former Kamloops IRS as reported by the Tk'emlúps te Secwépemc First Nation, Lorrie encountered a group of knitters on a Facebook group from Vancouver Island initiated by Jennifer Kent Symons. They were reconciling this difficult knowledge by knitting tiny orange sweaters as acts of remembrance and displaying them in public libraries. Lorrie brought the idea back to us at UBC. Soon, with colleague Dr. Kerry Renwick, we were engaged in a faculty-wide project aimed at knitting, crocheting, or beading as many orange sweaters as possible to create a permanent display in the education building on our campus. The Faculty of Education is a place where we consider the impacts of teaching, learning, and the roles of education in the broader society. Schools are supposed to be a place of learning where students are cared for and safe. We know that this has not been the case, particularly for Indigenous children who attended residential schools in Canada. Today, as educators of new teachers, we want to be sure that this knowledge of our history positively influences future teachers' awareness, actions, and attitudes so that no child will suffer as those did in the past.

As we sat together in workshops, teaching students, staff, and faculty to knit and crochet, we began to see multiple pedagogical implications for our work, particularly in nurturing inquiry projects for teachers specializing in many curricular areas. By sitting with the yarn in our hands and working stitches into tiny sweaters, we shared stories, observations, feelings and hopes. This is slow work and deliberate work that we do with care and intent. It doesn't matter that a beginner makes a mistake or slips a stitch; it is about the care and intention, the sharing of our work. Many of the students we first worked with were from the NITEP program (Indigenous Teacher Education Program).

Though almost all were new to knit and crochet work, they dug in and began with us and shared their thoughts and memories of family members who also do this kind of crafting. This is a work in progress and cannot be rushed.

SUMMING UP

The North is the last stop on our journey around the Medicine Wheel. We have moved together through consideration of the spirit in the East, bringing newness, self-knowledge, symbols, and abstractions. We travelled to the South and considered emotions, relationships, refinement, and discernment. In the West, we looked at the physical realm and considered how our bodies inform both curriculum and pedagogy and considered how sustaining our own bodies and the land as the body of our Mother is central to our work.

Our journey, though, is never really done. The path towards Indigenous education, just like the path of any relationship, is long and winding. It is recursive, and we will find ourselves returning to the Medicine Wheel time and again as we work, always seeking balance, always seeking enlightenment and connection. In the end, our practice as teachers is about doing our best for our students. Our students are the future, and we are responsible for getting them there. They are worth the work it takes.

Where to from here? Where are we now? Well, back at the beginning, ready for the next turn around the Medicine Wheel, but this time with a bit more understanding, sense of self, spirit, hope, curiosity, and direction. Our next chapter will take a look at things as a whole and see how this pedagogical approach of weaving Indigenous with Slow, of sowing Indigenous seeds into slow soil, plays out … or something like that.

WEAVING AND FINISHING

Our over and under with the weft, yarn travels and embraces the warp, becoming a sturdier and warmer cloth as our weaving progresses. This may seem like the end of a project, but it is really a careful, in-depth process. Stopping too soon will leave a half-woven cloth attached to a loom. Seeing a project through to its natural end, over, under, over, under, and so on, offers a particular kind of satisfaction. But, once the weaving is complete, it still needs to be properly finished. This means removing it from the loom, fixing the ends of the warp, so they do not unravel, and then washing the cloth. For a warm woollen blanket, this may mean a bit of a wash in warm soapy water. This results in a tiny bit of felting so that the warp and weft of the cloth are tight and do not separate when the cloth is draped or worn.

There is a specific technique for finishing each type of cloth. A wool cloth, a linen cloth, a cotton cloth, regardless of which one has been made, each needs finishing with either a wet method or a fulling method. Fulling is even a more vigorous method of finishing that involves some slamming of damp cloth onto a sturdy counter. The physicality of this method is rather enjoyable and is as playful as it is noisy. At first, it may seem counterintuitive to slam around a wet weaving that has taken many, many hours to create, but then it holds up. Not only is it okay, but it is also better than okay!

These final steps, the finishing and fulling, are comparable to the learning outcomes that a unit of study builds towards. But we know when we are planning student learning that they will ultimately learn far more than we could ever account for in a single lesson or unit.

Our metaphorical weaving of the warp and weft on our loom is, for the moment, complete. It has been crafted with our spirits, our hearts, hopes and minds. We have taken our weaving to our peers to slam around to help us with fulling (similar to gently felting) this cloth into a tightly woven and warm fabric. We are hopeful that it will stand up to the elements and keep us warm, and we can share it with our kin and our community.

In education terms, this fulling and finishing process is where one's completed project or work is celebrated, finished off well, and then shared, tested, and used. The use of this may be in the material world, as in a tangible object or learning artifact, or it may be an event, a reading, display, or conversation with an explanation. We now know that for learning to be *authentic*, it does not need to exist in the material world alone; it can exist in multiple realms, including the place of the heart, the spirit, the mind.

In describing the multiple curricular affordances of weaving, we hope we have illuminated similar possibilities for a variety of project-based approaches. And while weaving will not be accessible (or of interest) to everyone, we hope that you will have had a few ideas as you have read about projects that will be relevant to you and to your students. In polling our teacher friends, we were offered a wide range of project-based or inquiry learning ideas, one of which may resonate with you:

- School gardens,
- Community clean-up projects,
- Mural painting,
- School plays,
- Rummage sales,
- Welcome pole or canoe carving with Indigenous community members,
- Holiday craft sales,
- School dances,
- Robotics projects,
- Entrepreneurial projects, such as board game design,
- 4 H projects,
- Creating gift baskets for seniors,
- Rebuilding a car engine,
- Building bat boxes,
- Lunar New Year celebrations (such as Hobiyee),
- Community potlucks,
- Harvest festivals.

Science can help us to learn about the mechanics of fulling the wet-ted wool weaving transforms it into a warmer and possibly even a fuzzier blanket. But beyond any single subject, we can feel the learning with our hands, see it with our eyes, know it in our minds, care about it in our hearts, and wonder about it from a place inside we that we only can know of ourselves.

8

Pimoteh (Walking)

Leddy: When I was about twelve years old, my family moved from Saskatoon to Regina, Saskatchewan, for a brief period. It was late August, so we'd be arriving in time for the school year to begin, and I was feeling anxious about starting Grade 7 with strangers. I wanted to make a good impression, to seem like I was "with it," in-the-know, and cool to hang out with.

"Mom? Who is the mayor of Regina?" I asked at some point during the two-hour car ride.

"Why on earth do you need to know that?" she asked, peering curiously into the back seat, where I sat with my siblings.

"Well, you know, in case they ask us on the first day ... I don't want to look dumb," I replied with genuine earnestness.

"Oh, Shannon," she said, laughing kindly, "You don't have to know all of the answers on the first day!"

That kind of anxious keenness was a hallmark of all of my school experiences (other than for a brief period during high school, which remains clouded in the adolescent vagueness characteristic of puberty). I wanted to know all of the answers upfront, forgetting that the point of the school is to do some of that learning on-site and over time. As a more seasoned teacher, I now know too that learning involves making mistakes and that sometimes my students will know more than I do about this, that, and the other thing. We all learn together in this business.

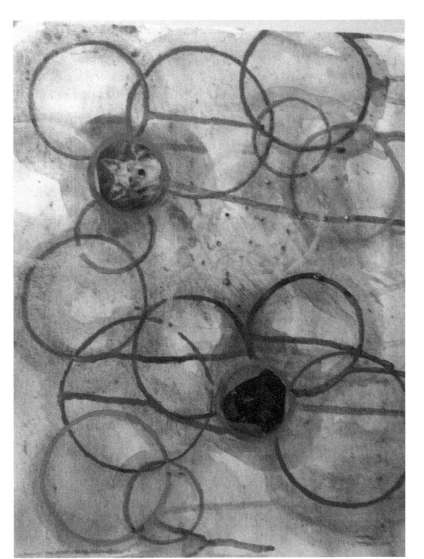

Figure 8.1. *Trickster Dance*, 2016.
Source: Courtesy of Shannon Leddy.

Teaching and learning is often a fraught business. Over the years, trends in curriculum and pedagogy have come and gone. New models for schooling have been tried and abandoned, or tried and found true but not widely popular. The Depression-era ideas of John Dewey are in some ways just now being applied – change takes time. And we certainly can't know everything at once. Just as we evolve as humans over time, gradually coming to understand ourselves and our world, education also evolves. At this particular moment in history, we have the opportunity to affect not just pedagogical or curricular change but an epistemological change in the way we conceive of and engage in education.

We have held the Medicine Wheel at the centre of our work, rooted in our understanding that our students need us to address more than just their intellects with our teaching. Experienced teachers know this to be true. Our students are also emotional, physical, and spiritual beings, and when we work with them, we need to make space for that. The Medicine Wheel also provides a useful framework onto which we can map both our curriculum and pedagogies so that we can ensure we are thinking of our students as whole human beings who live in the real world. In this light, for us as teachers, it is a tool of the intellect that helps us fulfill this responsibility. Including critical pedagogy that makes spaces for Indigenous epistemologies is another way we can nurture a more inclusive sense of what matters. In our role as educators, we are responsible to both our students and to the future.

We have held the First People's Principles of Learning (FNESC, 2008) at the centre of our work, recognizing that we teach people, not subjects. Education, as we increasingly understand, is not about the transmission of factoids and data. Instead, it is about preparing our students for the world they will inherit, not for the world as it once was. It is about helping them understand the connections between curriculum and their lives and ensuring that we hold that relationship at the centre of our work. As Shawn Wilson (2008) notes, "rather than viewing ourselves as being *in* relationship with other people or things, we *are* the relationships that we hold and are part of" (p. 80). We are all bound together on this planet, human and non-human creatures alike (see figure 8.1). We are made of the same material; we have the same needs. We *are* the spirit of this place. So, we need to help our students learn to honour the land, to live in a relationship with it, and to appreciate the web of interconnected relationships that form and sustain the network of life. We feel that the First People's Principles of Learning (FNESC, 2008) encourage a set of dispositions that are fundamentally decolonizing and which make space for non-Western ways of being and knowing.

We have also held Slow pedagogy at the centre of our work. We know that weaving Indigenous content and pedagogies into a Western paradigm will take time and patience, and the learning curve will be steeper for some than for others. Slow pedagogy gives us permission to do less but to do it more deeply. It invites us to dwell in the discomfort that can accompany decolonizing ourselves and our curriculum and pedagogies and to take the time necessary to process that discomfort. Slowing down gives us the opportunity to consider the ways in which navigating between Indigenous and Western paradigms is not an act of removal and replacement but rather an opportunity for reciprocity, the giving and taking of making space and making sense.

Over the weeks and months and years that we were developing this manuscript, we continued to hold the metaphor of weaving at the centre of our work, enjoying the way our ideas moved in and out through conversations, threads we picked up in readings reinforcing our experiences and instincts. Weaving, to us, is part of the physical aspect of our considerations here as an evocation of materiality. At some point, fairly early on in the history of modern humans, clever people around the world worked out how to transform fibres into fabric, whether with wool, grain stalks, cedar bark, or the webs of silkworms. The magnitude of learning between early coarse fibres and silk jacquard is considerable and lends further gravitas to our metaphor. The fabrics produced between the dawn of weaving and now have been used for warmth, shelter, transportation, comfort, and pleasure. Fabrics have been used to decorate, and they have been used to kill. And, like education itself, nearly every human life involves an experience of some kind of fabric at some point. But no weaver is born a master of their art.

Perhaps, now that you have come to the end of this book, you are somewhat disappointed to find that there were no lesson plans here, no prescriptions for learning and teaching, and no real concrete sequential instructions. And that's okay. If anything you have read here has resonated with you, then we trust that you will find your path. Decolonizing our teaching takes time, and effort, and persistence. Know that you may make mistakes, and be prepared to make amends when that happens. Know that you may fall down at some point along this path, and be prepared to find the courage you need to keep walking.

References

Absolon, K. (2010). Indigenous wholistic theory: A knowledge set for practice. *First Peoples Child & Family Review*, 5(2), 74–87. https://doi.org/10.7202/1068933ar

Adese, J. (2014). Spirit gifting: Ecological knowing in Métis life narratives. *Decolonization: Indigeneity, Education & Society*, 3(3), 48–66.

Ahenakew, C.R. (2017). Mapping and complicating conversations about Indigenous education. *Diaspora, Indigenous, and Minority Education*, 11(2), 80–91. https://doi.org/10.1080/15595692.2017.1278693

Alberta Regional Professional Development Consortium. (2018). *Weaving ways: Indigenous ways of knowing in classrooms and schools*. https://empoweringthespirit.ca/wp-content/uploads/2018/09/Weaving-Ways-Introductory-Document-10-09.pdf

Ames, M. (1994). *Cannibal tours, glass boxes, and the politics of interpretation*. UBC Press.

Archibald, J.A. (2008). *Indigenous storywork: Educating the heart, mind, body, and spirit*. UBC Press.

Arendt, H. (1958). *The human condition*. University of Chicago Press.

Association of Canadian Deans of Education. (2010). Accord on Indigenous education. https://csse-scee.ca/acde/wp-content/uploads/sites/7/2017/08/Accord-on-Indigenous-Education.pdf

Ayers, W., Kumashiro, K., Meiners, E.R., Quinn, T., & Stovall, D. (2017) *Teaching toward democracy*. Routledge. https://doi.org/10.4324/9781315536866

Bartlett, C., Marshall, M., & Marshall, A. (2012). Two-eyed seeing and other lessons learned within a co-learning journey of bringing together indigenous and mainstream knowledges and ways of knowing. *Journal of Environmental Studies and Sciences*, 2(4), 331–40. https://doi.org/10.1007/s13412-012-0086-8

Battiste, M. (1998). Enabling the autumn seed: Toward a decolonized approach to Aboriginal knowledge, language, and education. *Canadian Journal of Native Education, 22*(1), 16. https://doi.org/10.14288/cjne.v22i1.195792

Battiste, M. (2000). *Reclaiming Indigenous voice and vision.* UBC Press.

Battiste, M. (2013). *Decolonizing education: Nourishing the learning spirit.* Purich Publishing.

BC Hydro. (2018). *Constantly connected: BC's obsession with personal electronics and how it's shifting household electricity use.* https://www.bchydro.com/content/dam/BCHydro/customer-portal/documents/news-and-features/bchydro-report-constantly-connected-2018.pdf

BC Teachers' Council. (2019). *Professional standards for BC educators.* https://www2.gov.bc.ca/assets/gov/education/kindergarten-to-grade-12/teach/teacher-regulation/standards-for-educators/edu_standards.pdf

BC Teachers' Council. (2023). *Teacher Education program approval standards.* https://www2.gov.bc.ca/assets/gov/education/kindergarten-to-grade-12/teach/teacher-regulation/teacher-education-programs/tep_standards.pdf

Berg, M., & Seeber, B.K. (2017). *The slow professor: Challenging the culture of speed in the academy.* University of Toronto Press.

Birkerts, S. (1994). *The Gutenberg elegies: The fate of reading in an electronic age.* Faber and Faber.

Bloom, B.S. (Ed.). (1956). *Taxonomy of educational objectives, handbook 1: Cognitive domain.* Addison Wesley Publishing Company.

British Columbia. (2006). *Shared learnings: Integrating BC Aboriginal content K–10.* British Columbia, Aboriginal Education Enhancements Branch, British Columbia Ministry of Education. https://www2.gov.bc.ca/assets/gov/education/kindergarten-to-grade-12/teach/teaching-tools/aboriginal-education/shared_learning.pdf

British Columbia. (2015). *Aboriginal worldviews and perspectives in the classroom: Moving forward.* https://www2.gov.bc.ca/assets/gov/education/administration/kindergarten-to-grade-12/indigenous-education/awp_moving_forward.pdf

British Columbia, Ministry of Education. (2019). *BC curriculum comparison guide* (Rev. ed.). Ministry of Education.

Burgess, R. (2019). *Fibershed: Growing a movement of farmers, fashion activists, and makers for a new textile economy.* Chelsea Green Publishing.

Burtynsky, E., & Baichwal, J. (2008). *Manufactured landscapes.* British Film Institute.

Cajete, G. (1994). *Look to the mountain: An ecology of Indigenous education.* Kivaki Press.

Cajete, G. (2004). Philosophy of Native science. In A. Waters (Ed.), *American Indian thought* (pp. 45–57). Blackwell Publishing.

Calderon, D. (2014). Speaking back to Manifest Destinies: A land education-based approach to critical curriculum inquiry. *Environmental Education Research*, 20(1), 24–36. https://doi.org/10.1080/13504622.2013.865114

Canada, House of Commons. (2007, December 17). *Private members' business M-296 (First Nations children)*. 39th parliament, 2nd session, vote no. 27. https://www.ourcommons.ca/Members/en/votes/39/2/27

Canada, Royal Commission on Aboriginal Peoples, Dussault, R., & Erasmus, G. (1996). *Report of the Royal Commission on Aboriginal Peoples*. Canada Communication Group Publishing. https://hdl.handle.net/1974/6874

Canadian Teachers' Federation. (2015). *CTF survey on teachers' perspectives on Aboriginal education in public schools in Canada: Summary report*. https://eric.ed.gov/?id=ED602836

Carello, J., & Butler, L.D. (2015). Practicing what we teach: Trauma-informed educational practice. *Journal of Teaching in Social Work*, 35(3), 262–78. https://doi.org/10.1080/08841233.2015.1030059

Chrona, J. (2014). *Learning involves patience and time*. https://firstpeoplesprinciplesoflearning.wordpress.com/learning-involves-patience-and-time/

Cote-Meek, S. (2015). *Colonized classrooms: Racism, trauma and resistance in post-secondary education*. Fernwood Publishing.

Coulthard, G.S. (2014). *Red skin, white masks: Rejecting the colonial politics of recognition*. University of Minnesota Press. https://muse.jhu.edu/book/35470

Csikszentmihalyi, M. (1990). *Flow: The psychology of optimal experience*. Harper & Row.

Davidson, S.F., & Davidson, R. (2018). *Potlatch as pedagogy: Learning through ceremony*. Portage & Main Press.

Deer, F. (2019). Confronting Indigenous identities in transcultural contexts. In H. Tomlins-Jahnke, S. Styres, S. Lilley, & D. Zinga (Eds.), *Indigenous education: New directions in theory and practice* (1st ed., pp. 233–53). University of Alberta Press.

Dei, G.J.S. (1996). The role of Afrocentricity in the inclusive curriculum in Canadian schools. *Canadian Journal of Education/Revue canadienne de l'éducation*, 21(2), 170–86. https://doi.org/10.2307/1495088

de Leeuw, S., Greenwood, M., & Lindsay, N. (2013). Troubling good intentions. *Settler Colonial Studies*, 3(3–4), 381–94. https://doi.org/10.1080/2201473X.2013.810694

Deloria, V., Jr. (1969). *Custer died for your sins: An Indian manifesto*. University of Oklahoma Press.

Dion, S.D. (2007). Disrupting molded images: Identities, responsibilities and relationships – teachers and indigenous subject material. *Teaching Education, 18*(4), 329–42. https://doi.org/10.1080/10476210701687625

Dion, S.D. (2009). *Braiding histories: Learning from Aboriginal Peoples' experiences and perspectives.* UBC Press.

Donald, D. (2009). Forts, curriculum, and Indigenous Métissage: Imagining decolonization of Aboriginal-Canadian relations in educational contexts. *First Nations Perspectives, 2*(1), 1–24.

Donald, D. (2019). 5 homo economicus and forgetful curriculum. In H. Tomlins-Jahnke, S. Styres, S. Lilley, & D. Zinga (Eds.), *Indigenous education: New directions in theory and practice* (1st ed., pp. 103–25). University of Alberta Press.

First Nations Education Steering Committee. (2008). *Principles of learning First People* (poster). http://www.fnesc.ca/wp/wp-content/uploads/2015/09/PUB-LFP-POSTER-Principles-of-Learning-First-Peoples-poster-11x17.pdf

First Nations Education Steering Committee. (2018). *English First Peoples teacher's 10–12.* http://www.fnesc.ca/wp/wp-content/uploads/2018/08/PUBLICATION-LFP-EFP-10-12-FINAL-2018-08-13.pdf

Fixico, D.L. (2003). *The American Indian mind in a linear world: American Indian studies and traditional knowledge.* Routledge.

Freire, P. (1993). *Pedagogy of the oppressed.* Continuum. (Original work published 1970)

Freire, P. (1994). *Pedagogy of hope: Reliving pedagogy of the oppressed.* Continuum.

Friesen, J. (2019, June 26). As Indigenous land acknowledgements become the norm, critics question whether the gesture has lost its meaning. *The Globe and Mail.* https://www.theglobeandmail.com/canada/article-has-indigenous-land-acknowledgment-at-public-gatherings-become-an/

Gardner, H. (1983). *The theory of multiple intelligences.* Heinemann.

George, J., & Dei, S. (1996). The role of Afrocentricity in the inclusive curriculum in Canadian schools. *Canadian Journal of Education/Revue canadienne de l'éducation, 21*(2), 170–86. https://doi.org/10.2307/1495088

Graham, M.A. (2007). Art, ecology, and art education: Locating art education in a critical place-based pedagogy. *Studies in Art Education, 48*(4), 375–91. https://doi.org/10.1080/00393541.2007.11650115

Goldschmidt, M.L., Bachman, J.L., DiMattio, M.K., & Warker, J.A. (2016). Exploring slow teaching with an interdisciplinary community of practice. *Transformative Dialogues: Teaching & Learning Journal, 9*(1), 1–11.

Goulet, L.M., & Goulet, K.N. (2014). *Teaching each other: Nehinuw concepts and Indigenous pedagogies.* UBC Press.

Haig-Brown, C. (2010). Indigenous thought, appropriation, and non-Aboriginal people. *Canadian Journal of Education/Revue canadienne de l'éducation, 33*(4), 925–50.

Hatcher, A., Bartlett, C., Marshall, A., & Marshall, M. (2009). Two-eyed seeing in the classroom environment: Concepts, approaches, and challenges. *Canadian Journal of Science, Mathematics and Technology Education, 9*(3), 141–53. https://doi.org/10.1080/14926150903118342

Holmes, K., & Leggo, C. (2019). Places of the heart. In E. Lyle (Ed.), *Identity landscapes, contemplating place and the construction of self* (pp. 281–96). Brill & Sense.

Holt, M. (2002). It's time to start the slow school movement. *Phi Delta Kappan, 84*(4), 264–71. https://doi.org/10.1177/003172170208400404

Honoré, C. (2004). *In praise of slow: Challenging the cult of speed.* Vintage Canada.

Honoré, C. (2013). *The slow fix: Solve problems, work smarter, and live better in a world addicted to speed.* HarperOne.

hooks, b. (1994). *Teaching to transgress: Education as the practice of freedom.* Routledge.

hooks, b. (2003). *Teaching community: A pedagogy of hope.* Routledge.

Ingold, T. (2017). *Anthropology and/as education.* Routledge.

Jones Brayboy, B.M., & Maughan, E. (2009). Indigenous knowledges and the story of the bean. *Harvard Educational Review, 79*(1), 1–21. https://doi.org/10.17763/haer.79.1.l0u6435086352229

King, T. (2003). *The truth about stories: A Native narrative.* House of Anansi.

King, T. (2012). *The inconvenient Indian illustrated: A curious account of Native people in North America.* Doubleday Canada.

Kirkness, V.J. (1999). Aboriginal education in Canada: A retrospective and a prospective. *Journal of American Indian Education, 39*(1), 14–30.

Kirkness, V.J., & Barnhardt, R. (1991). First Nations and higher education: The four R's – respect, relevance, reciprocity, responsibility. *Journal of American Indian Education, 30*(3), 1–15.

LaFever, M. (2016). Switching from Bloom to the Medicine Wheel: Creating learning outcomes that support Indigenous ways of knowing in post-secondary education. *Intercultural Education, 27*(5), 409–24. https://doi.org/10.1080/14675986.2016.1240496

Lane, P., Jr., Bopp, J., Bopp, M., & Brown, L. (1984). *The sacred tree.* Lotus Press.

Laufer, P. (2011). *Slow news: A manifesto for the critical news consumer.* Oregon State University Press

Leddy, S. (2018). In a good way: Reflecting on humour in Indigenous education. *Journal of the Canadian Association for Curriculum Studies, 16*(2), 10–20.

Leddy, S., & O'Neill, S. (2022). Learning to see: Phenomenological art inquiry in teacher education. *International Journal of Education & the Arts, 23*(9). https://doi.org/10.26209/ijea23n9

Lewis, H.R. (2004). *Slow down: Getting more out of Harvard by doing less.* https://lewis.seas.harvard.edu/files/harrylewis/files/slowdown2004_0.pdf

Lipson, E. (2012). The slow cloth manifesto: An alternative to the politics of production. *Textile Society of America Symposium Proceedings,* 711. http://digitalcommons.unl.edu/tsaconf/711

Little Bear, L. (2000). Jagged worldviews colliding. In M. Battiste (Ed.), *Reclaiming Indigenous voice and vision* (pp. 77–85). UBC Press.

Lowman, E.B., & Barker, A.J. (2015). *Settler: Identity and colonialism in 21st century Canada*. Fernwood Publishing.

McDonald, M. (2014, September 10). *How to grow zucchini*. Westcoast Seeds. https://www.westcoastseeds.com/blogs/how-to-grow/grow-zucchini

McIlvride, D., & Williams, R. (Directors). (2017). *RiverBlue* [Film]. Collective Eye Films.

Menzies, H. (2005). *No time: Stress and the crisis of modern life*. Douglas & McIntyre.

Menzies, H., & Newson, J. (2007). No time to think: Academics' life in the globally wired university. *Time & Society, 16*(1), 83–98. https://doi.org/10.1177/0961463X07074103

Mezirow, J. (2009). Transformative learning theory. In J. Mezirow & E.W. Taylor (Eds.), *Transformative learning in practice: Insights from community, workplace, and higher education* (pp. 18–32). John Wiley & Sons.

Michell, H. (2018). *Land-based education: Embracing the rhythms of the earth from an Indigenous perspective*. Charlton Publishing.

Mikics, D. (2013). *Slow reading in a hurried age*. Harvard University Press.

Miller, L. (1995). *Learning to be proud: First Nations women's stories of learning, teaching, art and culture* [Master's thesis, University of British Columbia]. UBC Theses and Dissertations. https://doi.org/10.14288/1.0054767

Miller, L., Aden, A.O., Mohamed, J.A., Hussein, Z.B., & Okello, A.O. (2019). The ripple effects when a refugee camp becomes a university town: University teacher education in Dadaab, Kenya. *Journal of Educational Research and Innovation, 7*(1). 1–17, Article 7. https://digscholarship.unco.edu/jeri/vol7/iss1/7

Nakamura, J., & Csikszentmihalyi, M. (2002). The concept of flow. In C.R. Snyder & S.J. Lopez (Eds.), *Handbook of positive psychology* (pp. 89–105). Oxford University Press.

Nakamura, J., & Csikszentmihalyi, M. (2014). The concept of flow. In M. Csikszentmihalyi (Ed.), *Flow and the foundations of positive psychology: The collected works of Mihaly Csikszentmihalyi*. Springer. https://doi.org/10.1007/978-94-017-9088-8_16

Nancy, J. (2000). *Being singular plural*. Stanford University Press.

National Inquiry into Missing and Murdered Indigenous Women and Girls. (2019). *Reclaiming power and place: The final report of the national inquiry into missing and murdered Indigenous women and girls*. National Inquiry into Missing and Murdered Indigenous Women and Girls. https://canadacommons.ca/artifacts/1196236/reclaiming-power-and-place/1749360/

Oleman, G. (2019). *Gerry Oleman on Indigenous education and wellbeing* [Video]. https://indigenizinglearning.educ.ubc.ca/curriculum-bundles/

Olsen, S. (2010). *Working with wool: A Coast Salish legacy and the Cowichan sweater*. Sono Nis Press.

Parent, A. (2011). "Keep us coming back for more": Urban Aboriginal youth speak about wholistic education. *Canadian Journal of Native Education*, *34*(1), 28–48. https://doi.org/10.14288/cjne.v34i1.196658

Payne, P. (2005). "Ways of Doing," Learning, teaching, and researching. *Canadian Journal of Environmental Education*, *10*(1), 108–24.

Payne, P.G., & Wattchow, B. (2009). Phenomenological deconstruction, slow pedagogy, and the corporeal turn in wild environmental/outdoor education. *Canadian Journal of Environmental Education*, *14*(1), 15–32.

Petrini, C., Furlan, C., & Hunt, J. (2007). *Slow food nation: Why our food should be good, clean, and fair*. Rizzoli Ex Libris.

Pihama, L., Smith, L.T., Te Nana, R., Cameron, N., Mataki, T., Skipper, H., & Southey, K. (2017). Investigating Māori approaches to trauma-informed care. *Journal of Indigenous Wellbeing*, *2*(3), 18–31.

Reagan, P. (2010). *Unsettling the settler within*. UBC Press.

Regnier, R. (1994). The sacred circle: A process pedagogy of healing. *Interchange*, *25*(2), 129–44. https://doi.org/10.1007/BF01534540

Restoule, J.-P. & Nardozzi, A. (2019). Exploring teacher candidate resistance to Indigenous content in a teacher education program. In H. Tomlins-Jahnke, S. Styres, S. Lilley, & D. Zinga (Eds.), *Indigenous education: New directions in theory and practice* (1st ed., pp. 311–37). University of Alberta Press.

Sanford, K., Williams, L., Hopper, T., & McGregor, C. (2012). Indigenous principles informing teacher education: What we have learned. *Education*, *18*(2), 1–12. https://doi.org/10.37119/ojs2012.v18i2.61

Sauvé, L. (2005). Currents in environmental education: Mapping a complex and evolving pedagogical field. *Canadian Journal of Environmental Education*, *10*(1), 11–37.

Schick, C., & St. Denis, V. (2005). Troubling national discourses in anti-racist curricular planning. *Canadian Journal of Education/Revue canadienne de l'éducation*, *28*(3), 295–317. https://doi.org/10.2307/4126472

Seawright, G. (2014). Settler traditions of place: Making explicit the epistemological legacy of White supremacy and settler colonialism for place-based education. *Educational Studies*, *50*(6), 554–72. https://doi.org/10.1080/00131946.2014.965938

Shahjahan, R.A. (2015). Being "lazy" and slowing down: Toward decolonizing time, our body, and pedagogy. *Educational Philosophy and Theory*, *47*(5), 488–501. https://doi.org/10.1080/00131857.2014.880645

Shaw, P., Cole, B., & Russell J. (2013). Determining our own tempos. *To Improve the Academy*, *32*(1), 319–34. https://doi.org/10.1002/j.2334-4822.2013.tb00713.x

Sparrow, D. (1998). A journey. In I. Bachmann & R. Scheuing (Eds.). *Material matters: The art and culture of contemporary textiles* (pp. 149–56). YYZ Books.

St. Denis, V., & Schick, C. (2003). What makes anti-racist pedagogy in teacher education difficult? Three popular ideological assumptions. *Alberta*

Journal of Educational Research, 49(1), 55–69. https://doi.org/10.11575/ajer.v49i1.54959

Stein, S. (2020). "Truth before reconciliation": The difficulties of transforming higher education in settler colonial contexts. *Higher Education Research & Development, 39*(1), 156–70. https://doi.org/10.1080/07294360.2019.1666255

Sterzuk, A., & Mulholland, V. (2011). Creepy White gaze: Rethinking the diorama as a pedagogical activity. *Alberta Journal of Educational Research, 57*(1), 16–27. https://doi.org/10.11575/ajer.v57i1.55452

Taylor, Drew Hayden. (2006). *Me funny*. Douglas & McIntyre.

Thiessen, H. (2017). *Slow knitting: A journey from sheep to skein to stitch*. Abrams.

Thom, J. (2019). *Slow teaching: On finding calm, clarity and impact in the classroom*. John Catt Educational.

Thomas, R. (2016, June 13). *Etuaptmumk: Two-eyed seeing* [Video]. TEDxNSCC Waterfront. YouTube. https://youtu.be/bA9EwcFbVfg

Tomlins-Jahnke, H. (2019). Contested spaces. In H. Tomlins-Jahnke, S. Styres, S. Lilley, & D. Zinga (Eds.), *Indigenous education: New directions in theory and practice* (1st ed., pp. 83–102). University of Alberta Press.

Trinkwon, M.L. (2010). Locating textile arts pedagogy: Do we ever settle? *Textile Society of America Symposium Proceedings*, 55. https://digitalcommons.unl.edu/tsaconf/55

Truth and Reconciliation Commission of Canada. (2015a). *Canada's residential schools: The final report of the Truth and Reconciliation Commission of Canada* (Vol. 1). McGill-Queen's University Press.

Truth and Reconciliation Commission of Canada. (2015b). *Canada's residential schools: Missing children and unmarked burials – The final report of the truth and reconciliation commission of Canada* (Vol. 4). McGill-Queen's University Press.

Truth and Reconciliation Commission of Canada. (2015c). *Truth and Reconciliation Commission of Canada: Calls to action*. TRC. https://www2.gov.bc.ca/assets/gov/british-columbians-our-governments/indigenous-people/aboriginal-peoples-documents/calls_to_action_english2.pdf

Tuck, E., & Yang, K.W. (2012). Decolonization is not a metaphor. *Decolonization: Indigeneity, Education & Society, 1*(1), 1–40. https://jps.library.utoronto.ca/index.php/des/article/view/18630

van der Wey, D. (2007). Coalescing in cohorts: Building coalitions in First Nations education. *Canadian Journal of Education/Revue canadienne de l'éducation, 30*(4), 989–1014. https://doi.org/10.2307/20466676

Vizenor, G. (Ed.). (2008). *Survivance: Narratives of native presence*. University of Nebraska Press.

Wagamese, R. (2008). *One Native life*. Douglas & McIntyre.

Wagamese, R. (2019). *One drum: Stories and ceremonies for a planet*. Douglas & McIntyre.

Wall-Kimmerer, R. (2013). *Braiding sweetgrass: Indigenous wisdom, scientific knowledge and the teachings of plants*. Milkweed Editions.

Watson, J. (2001). Social constructivism in the classroom. *Support for Learning*, *16*(3), 140–7. https://doi.org/10.1111/1467-9604.00206

Wattchow, B. (2001). A pedagogy of production: Craft, technology and outdoor education. *Australian Journal of Outdoor Education*, *5*(2), 19–28. https://doi.org/10.1007/BF03400730

Weems, L. (2016). Decolonialization at its intersections. In M.A. Peters (Ed.), *Encyclopedia of educational philosophy and theory* (pp. 253–57). https://doi.org/10.1007/978-981-287-532-7_532-1

Wellesley-Smith, C. (2015). *Slow stitch: Mindful and contemplative textile art*. Pavilion Books.

Wildcat, M., McDonald, M., Irlbacher-Fox, S., & Coulthard, G. (2014). Learning from the land: Indigenous land based pedagogy and decolonization. *Decolonization: Indigeneity, Education & Society*, *3*(3), I–XV. https://jps.library.utoronto.ca/index.php/des/article/view/22248

Wilson, S. (2008). Research is ceremony. *Indigenous research methods*. Fernwood Publishing.

Yazzie, R. (2000). Indigenous peoples and postcolonial colonialism. In M. Battiste (Ed.), *Reclaiming Indigenous voice and vision* (pp. 39–49). UBC Press.

Ylijoki, O.-H., & Mäntylä, H. (2003). Conflicting time perspectives in academic work. *Time & Society*, *2*(1), 55–78. https://doi.org/10.1177/0961463X03012001364

Index

Note: Page numbers in *italics* indicate a figure.

Printed and bound by CPI Group (UK) Ltd, Croydon, CR0 4YY

13/04/2025

14656519-0005